Faith Maps

Faith Maps

Ten religious explorers from Newman to Joseph Ratzinger

Michael Paul Gallagher SJ

Paulist Press
New York/Mahwah, N.J.

First published in 2010 by
Darton, Longman and Todd Ltd
1 Spencer Court
140–142 Wandsworth High Street
London SW18 4JJ

Library of Congress Control Number: 2010927348

ISBN: 978-0-8091-4698-7

North American edition published in 2010 by

Paulist Press, Inc.
997 Macarthur Boulevard
Mahwah, New Jersey, 07430
United States of America
www.paulistpress.com

Phototypeset by Kerrypress Ltd., Luton, Bedfordshire, UK
Printed and bound by Thomson Litho, East Kilbride, Scotland.

Contents

Introduction
Learning from the Giants

Instructions for living a life:

> *Pay attention.*
> *Be astonished*
> *Tell about it.*

(Mary Oliver, *Red Bird*)

I have no idea how many hours of my life have been devoted to books. Reading was a major part of my village childhood, in the years before television. What began with Enid Blyton ended up with Balthasar, with years of Bronte, Beckett and Bellow in between. After the village and secondary school came universities and studies of literature. That in turn led to some twenty years as a lecturer in literature in University College, Dublin. Because I was also a Jesuit priest that long period of contact with students brought me towards theology. Listening to them was like living in the future: I learned that the securities of traditional faith were in deep trouble, not because of intellectual difficulties but because of a new culture, involving a whole cluster of changed assumptions about life. I developed a passion for making sense of faith for this new world.

Life then took me away from Ireland. The plan was to go to Paraguay but I ended up in Rome, where after five years in the Vatican's Council for Culture, I became professor of theology in the Gregorian University. In spite of having a doctorate in theology, my background was different from most of my colleagues. I realised that my horizon had been shaped, slowly but permanently, by all those years in literature and in a state university. At first it seemed a handicap. I simply did not have the expertise in theology that was typical of my fellow professors. But after a time I realised that what life had given me could help me, and my students, to face questions of faith in a more imaginative way. With a sensibility shaped by literature and by years of exposure to an emerging culture, I read theology with different eyes. I plunged into the great

thinkers of the twentieth century, seeking to make them understandable for people I have known. And that, quite simply, is the
origin of this book.

Harvesting for others

What have I learned in all these years of reading about religion, of
studying or teaching theology, and, perhaps more importantly, of
trying to pray each day of my life? What have I discovered that
could be communicated to others, to those who have not hade my
chances to enquire and reflect? These pages are an attempt to
harvest my reading and thinking and to make it available for people
in search of God, even for those many honest friends who tell me
that God is not so much incredible, as unreal – simply off their
map. I first wanted to call this book 'Translating the Giants' but the
publishers advised me to find a less obscure title. My idea was (and
is) to translate the great tradition of theology for those who have
not been able to visit these fields at any length. My life, as I said, has
pushed me into this field, where I have spent those countless hours
learning from the giants, and I now hope to serve others by
gathering the fruits of those explorations for them.

So the purpose of this book is quite straightforward. I hope to
offer others the fruits of my reflecting on faith, a personal adventure that has lasted half a century. More specifically I want to
gather from the wisdom of ten major writers, and to let their
wisdom reach people who cannot devote so much time to reading.
The aim is to capture what these 'giants' say in today's language and
in a non-academic way. I am convinced that many people, whether
they think of themselves as religious believers or not, are looking
for nourishment of this kind – a mixture of intelligent and spiritual
wavelengths. Each of the ten authors has explored questions of
meaning and of faith, with depth and creativity, but most of them
can, at least at first, seem unreadable for a non-specialist public. My
objective is to make their riches accessible for more people.

The focus is not simply the existence of God. That is important,
but it is a narrower topic. Faith is something else. It involves the
whole of me, not just the level that can argue about the possibility
of God. It involves the whole story of God, as revealed in Jesus

Christ, not just some explanation of the universe. I recall a remark by an Irish journalist to the effect that in pubs you can sometimes hear arguments about God or the Church, but hardly ever about Jesus Christ. Pub discourse on religion tends to stay on the surface. But what I want to explore here takes us into another logic and on to another wavelength. External arguments about some kind of supernatural force (sometimes wrongly called 'God') will never do justice to real faith. It is only from within our hearts, our minds, and our humble searching, that we can find a worthy road. (All the rest is Richard Dawkins' territory.)

The book is entitled 'Faith Maps' in the sense that each chapter takes a major religious thinker and asks how he or she would point us in the direction of Christian faith. The focus will be more on how we can move towards the possibility of religious belief, and less on the content of what we believe. I realise, as I said, that many of my unbelieving friends can experience this God-talk as a language for which they have no dictionary, no grammar. I would ask them simply to get in touch with their own deeper questions, and then, through browsing in these pages, they might begin to appreciate the long tradition of pondering the strangeness and the surprise called God. How can we do justice to that perennial drama of desire and of discovery in a way that makes sense for today? In the first section of each chapter, a major explorer will be introduced in his or her own words. After summarising how they tried to understand the path towards faith, in most of the chapters I attempt a more experimental wavelength, trying to answer the question: what would this thinker say to us today? In eight of the chapters I dare to create an imaginary monologue, as if spoken by one of the 'giants' now. Indeed, readers less accustomed to theology could find it easier to read these sections first (they occur in every chapter except those dealing with Dorothee Soelle and Joseph Ratzinger, where a different second half seemed more suitable).

The context of today

What is this 'today'? How can we describe it? Let me evoke a few memories of a world that no longer exists. At least in our Western world, who now grows up playing on a small village street, or without television and internet? And who grows up today with religion as a seemingly natural part of life, from family prayer to more solemn moments in the parish church, such as Benediction, or missions, or high Mass? 'We were as Danes in Denmark all day long': a line from Wallace Stevens sums it all up. I am thinking of my childhood in Ireland, but it applies to the whole world. Sixty or more years ago, most people lived with a village-style mentality, even in the middle of cities like New York. This was true of Catholics in their parishes, but surely also of other religious believers, Christian or not. Believing and belonging went hand in hand.

Today it is rare for a child to experience such a smooth and untroubled religious inheritance. Everywhere in the Western world the Church has suffered a massive loss of ground. It is seldom at the centre of people's lives. In today's complexity it is just one of many potential sources of meaning, and perhaps not a very attractive one at that. For huge numbers of the younger generation what the Church offers – in terms of teaching, or worship, or spiritual image – rings strange, and sometimes even hollow and dishonest. Perhaps they had some contact in childhood, with memorable moments such as first communion (an event easily hijacked into a consumerist orgy), but once adolescence comes the language of Church can seem utterly alien. Where will they find roads that lead towards Christian faith? Probably not through sacraments or liturgy, at least as a first step. These are high expressions, rich when they are real, but empty when they have no personal basis in the 'religious imagination' (a key expression from Newman). If the Church puts all its pastoral eggs in the sacramental basket, then (to mix metaphors) it puts the cart before the horse. People need to discover their souls first, to retrieve the desires that a dominant lifestyle can smother. Then they might be able to awaken to the surprise of the Gospel. This is what the 'new evangelisation' (so encouraged by Pope John Paul II) might mean: it can no longer be achieved through the 'old sacramentalisation' approach which fitted perfectly with my village culture.

This book assumes the death of a stable tradition and the arrival of a complex culture. If 'context conditions consciousness', as Marxists used to say, it is obvious that this radically changed world has a huge impact on the possibility of religious faith. In this new situation very few people simply inherit the faith of their parents. Even the ordinary expression 'transmission of faith' seems too self-confident, too automatic and out of date. We need a different agenda of spiritual nourishment and reflection, and the authors explored in these chapters have tried to provide some of its essential ingredients. In spite of their many differences, they share a common goal to re-think and re-present faith in ways that can reach people of today.

How far can a book help people in their searching? Reading can be a lonely activity, but readers of these pages are invited to do so meditatively. A merely heady approach will never discover the core of faith – as love offered and accepted. It is a 'yes' to a 'yes', where God's eternal 'yes' to us comes first and our unsteady 'yes' of recognition comes later. So I will try to write in a spirit of reverence, hoping to be read in a spirit of openness to the imagination of God. Yes, that is what we are talking about: how God invites us to imagine our lives as grounded in a Love beyond all imagining.

Nearly half-a-century ago, the Second Vatican Council produced the first serious treatment of atheism in church history. After intense debate the Council opted for an approach rooted in dialogue and self-questioning. It abandoned the previous tendency to treat atheism just as a dangerous philosophical error or else as an unjust political system. Even today the opening words of the sections dealing with unbelief are remarkable: they speak three times of love and then introduce the phenomenon of atheism as an incapacity to recognise the biblical revelation of love. Thus atheism is viewed not as a theoretical rejection of a distant God but as an existential issue involving a missed relationship, an unrecognised invitation.

Here is a simplified paraphrase of that opening paragraph (*Gaudium et Spes*, 19).

> Our highest human goal is to encounter God. We are
> born from love, kept alive by love, and fullness of life
> comes when we recognise this love and freely embrace it.
> But many people today, sadly, cannot glimpse or perceive
> this intimate calling. And therefore atheism has become
> one of the most serious issues of our time.

In an eloquent speech to close the Council, Pope Paul VI singled out this new tone concerning faith and unbelief:

> 'Secular humanism showed itself in all its stature and challenged the Council ... What happened? A conflict, a struggle, a condemnation? That could have been possible but it did not happen. The ancient story of the Samaritan became the model of the spirituality of the Council. A huge sympathy took over ... So you modern humanists, even though you reject transcendence, we ask you to recognise our new humanism, because we too, we more than anyone, are cultivators of humanity.'

The ten authors visited in these pages explore the issue of faith in this spirit of dialogue and sympathy (even those who lived before the Council). They are intensely aware that doctrinal or abstract approaches can fail to meet people where they are today. They realise that many people, including themselves at times, experience painful confusion over ultimate meaning, over church life, and over the possibility of God. The challenge of a fragmented culture spurs them to try to make sense of faith for new situations. It also underlies my attempt to translate these giants, in the hope of helping people to discover or rediscover the treasure trail towards a faith that can transform everything.

1

John Henry Newman: the journey of the self

Even in his own day Cardinal Newman was seen as one of the giants of his time. When he died at nearly ninety years of age, hundreds of tributes were published in British newspapers and journals, including those who seldom paid attention to Church affairs. Many of those obituaries praised his prose style (just as James Joyce was later to admit to feeling jealous of Newman's "silver-veined" language). But the accolades of 1890 also recognised that a great spiritual figure had died, someone who had brought new wisdom to the question of religious commitment. For instance this surprisingly generous comment appeared in the *Freethinker*, a periodical for atheists:

> Newman is the purest stylist and the greatest theologian in our language. His perfect eloquence charmed his worst opponents ... a confirmed Atheist might almost regret the necessity of differing from him ... "Here," we said to ourselves, "is one who is more than a Catholic, more than a theologian; one who has lived an intense inner life, who understands the human heart as few have understood it, who follows the subtlest workings of the human mind, who helps the reader to understand himself."

All these qualities so admired in Newman were in fact dedicated towards one central goal. The guiding passion of his long life was to make sense of the Christian vision for an age when belief in God seemed in deep trouble. Always alert to the currents of the culture around him, Newman devoted much energy to how we arrive at faith, and he did this in many forms, ranging from sermons to philosophical reflections, and from autobiography to poetry and novels. The originality of his approach has influenced reflection on religious belief ever since and he remains the precursor of what is best in theology of faith during the last century or so. He liked to say that the best evidence for God lies within us, and so he moved the agenda away from external arguments to personal and pre-

rational areas of moral and spiritual readiness. Without ever falling
into subjectivism, he explored the inner movements of the self
towards truth. Indeed the then Cardinal Ratzinger commented (in
1991) that no theologian since Augustine had paid so much
attention to the human subject.

Three cultural challenges

The young Newman found himself facing three major challenges
to faith. First of all, there was the narrow rationalism associated
with scientific verification. If faith was to be defended, in Newman's view, reason would need to retrieve its full existential range,
not simply as a 'paper logic' but as a movement of the whole person.
Faith is never, he insisted, merely a conclusion of the mind: it
involves a Word of revelation that encounters us in the depths of
our humanity, and thus initiates an adventure of change that lasts a
lifetime.

Secondly, there was what he called 'liberalism'. He became a
great proponent of 'liberal education', but what he opposed as
liberalism in religion was the widespread idea that 'there is no
positive truth in religion' (words he used when accepting his
nomination as Cardinal at the age of 78). He was vehemently
opposed to the tendency of his time to reduce faith to a matter of
private opinion, rather like taste in music. One of his early poems is
entitled 'Liberalism' and expresses the danger in these words:

> Ye cannot halve the Gospel of God's grace;
> Men of presumptuous heart!

The liberals, according to these verses of 1833, interpreted religion
in a merely humanistic way as a source of peace or good-will, and so
they avoided the 'dread depths of grace'. Such fashionable vagueness, masquerading as tolerance, was attractive for the comfortable
middle-class culture of Victorian England. Human criteria
became the touchstone of truth. When woolly thinking and selfish
attitudes went together, it produced a soft version of the Gospel
which he called 'the religion of the day'. But faith, in his view, can
never be made to measure for the ego; on the contrary, it will entail
the erosion of all our complacencies.

The third challenge came from within the religious world itself. Perhaps under the influence of the Romantic movement in poetry and art, revival movements gave great emphasis to religious feeling and to emotional experiences of conversion. Newman, as will be seen, came to value the role of 'heart', 'imagination' and 'affections' in the life of faith, but he remained suspicious of an exaggerated focus on religious sentiment. It risked forgetting the rich history of the Church, the long tradition of theological reflection, as well as the centrality of sacramental life. Faith, therefore, should not be reduced to subjective intensity; the Gospel is very different – a definite and gradual revelation of the mystery of Jesus.

Faced with these challenges, Newman sought to deepen the agenda of thinking about faith and to do justice to the full range of Christian experience. He wanted to help people to recognise the simplicity and yet the complexity of belief. On the one hand, to trust what others tell us is a most normal and everyday necessity. On the other, to arrive at Christian belief in God involves more than what he called 'notional assent': it goes beyond any intellectual or theoretical acceptance of the existence of God. Instead it needs to be profoundly personal and therefore requires 'real assent' in the sense of an existential recognition of God that changes us. Newman insisted on the ordinariness of *how* we believe and on the extraordinariness of *what* we believe: 'we are acting on trust every hour of our lives … it is the things believed, not the act of believing them, which is peculiar to religion' (*PPS*, I, 191).

Focus on disposition and conscience

Newman preached those words as a young Anglican minister of 28. Ten years later he began a series of five sermons at Oxford University on the general theme of faith and reason. They were preached at various times between 1839 and 1841 and became famous at that time. Some of his hearers, such as the poet Matthew Arnold, recalled in later years the sheer music of his voice and the hypnotic quality of attentiveness induced by his reflections. These five texts, more lectures than sermons by today's standards, offer us Newman's anthropology of faith. His main focus is on crucial personal attitudes that leave us open or else closed to the possibility

of Christian believing. Again and again he distanced himself from
the dominant Oxford school of 'evidences', an approach that tried
to prove the existence of God through the order of the natural
universe. He thought that they were, so to speak, barking up the
wrong tree. Instead Newman chose a much more psychological
route, with an emphasis on human interiority. He was by temperament highly introspective and he saw our lived dispositions as
much more relevant for faith than the more externalist arguments
of his fellow academics. He was not interested in proofs for the
existence of God but in certain personal attitudes that an individual
will need to have in order to arrive at faith.

This emphasis may have originated during his years as a student
at Oxford, when he had a series of fruitless debates with his
younger brother Charles, who had become an atheist. We know
something of these exchanges from a series of eight letters that
have survived, and which stress certain inner qualities needed for
any growth from unbelief towards faith. He told his brother
bluntly, 'you are not in a state of mind to listen to argument of any
kind'. Since 'internal evidence depends a great deal on moral
feeling', rejection of faith often arises 'from a fault of the heart, not
of the intellect'. He saw his brother as blocked by a prejudice
against faith: when it comes to 'religious subjects' we tend to see
everything 'through the glass of previous habits' (*LD*, I, 212–226).
As Newman was to repeat in later years, a typical source of refusal
to believe in God lies in excessive self-trust, in a cold and proud
rejection of any dependence and in an avoidance of one's own
conscience. That unsuccessful attempt to persuade his brother of
the truth of Christianity probably confirmed Newman in his
misgivings about external approaches. More positively, it gave him
confidence in his natural tendency to give special attention to the
spiritual dispositions of individuals or indeed of a whole culture.

This focus on the inner or moral attitudes necessary for faith put
Newman at odds with the dominant apologetics of his time – both
as an Anglican and as a Catholic. In his *Apologia pro Vita Sua*,
written a decade after his conversion, he was quite outspoken about
his unease with traditional proofs of the existence of God. In a
remarkable passage he points to the grounds of his religious security as lying within his experience of conscience:

Starting then with the being of a God, (which, as I have said, is as certain to me as the certainty of my own existence ...) I look out of myself into the world of men, and there I see a sight which fills me with unspeakable distress. The world seems simply to give the lie to that great truth, of which my whole being is so full ... If I looked into a mirror, and did not see my face, I should have the sort of feeling which actually comes upon me, when I look into this living busy world, and see no reflexion of its Creator ... Were it not for this voice, speaking so clearly in my conscience and my heart, I should be an atheist ... I am far from denying the real force of the arguments in proof of a God, drawn from the general facts of human society and the course of history, but these do not warm me or enlighten me; they do not take away the winter of my desolation, or make the buds unfold and the leaves grow within me, and my moral being rejoice. (*A*, 241).

The University Sermons and 'antecedent probability'

That final sentence is revealing. After expressing his rather tragic vision of the world, he suggests that genuine faith is best known by its fruits, including a steady enlargement of inner life and some sense of joy. He had elaborated this approach more than a decade earlier in his university sermons. Interestingly, after Newman's conversion to Catholicism, he worried that the Roman authorities might not appreciate these Oxford texts. During his stay in Rome in 1846 he found that the dominant thinking on faith there was conceptual and impersonal – rather like the school of external evidence that he had resisted among his fellow Anglicans. In a letter written from Rome in 1847 he commented that his most original insight involved his focus on 'antecedent probability'. That had been a frequent expression in his university sermons and, although it can at first seem complicated, in reality it is quite simple: 'antecedent probability' draws attention to what precedes all explicit expression. We speak today of the pre-conceptual area of reflection. Prior to our stated beliefs or formulated reasoning about

faith there is the whole area of our fundamental attitudes. In this
hidden field of our previous dispositions Newman located the
'probability' (or not) of our readiness for faith.

As he put it in a university sermon, the 'fatal error' of secular
thinking is to judge 'religious truth without preparation of heart'
(*US*, X, 43). And he added his critique of a cold intellectualism in
apologetics: 'in the schools of the world the ways towards Truth are
considered high roads open to all men, however disposed, at all
times. Truth is to be approached without homage' (*US*, X, 42). This
is Newman in a nutshell: any fruitful path towards faith will always
need a certain spiritual receptivity as opposed to arrogant distance;
in his view the religious horizon becomes real, not though clever
argumentation, but only when 'the heart is alive' (*US*, X, 44).
Without this quality of honest searching we cannot arrive at the
'active recognition' that is faith and that brings its own special
certitude (*GA*, 345). In other words Newman had the courage to
underline what the intellectual culture then and now tended to
neglect: that in matters of faith what can be formally thought out is
less important than dispositions, desires and states of mind. To
repeat: openness for faith, in his view, entailed certain moral attitudes within the person, and if these are not present all our efforts at
making faith intellectually credible can fall on stony ground.

Two years after his conversion to Catholicism, Newman prepared an introduction for a possible French edition of his university
sermons, except that he wrote it in Latin. There we find the
following sentence: '*Praeambula fidei in individuis non cadunt sub
scientiam*': the preambles of faith in individuals do not fall into the
sphere of science. A freer translation could be: the roads that
prepare people for faith cannot be reduced to empirical analysis.
Perhaps Newman saw himself as an intellectual version of John the
Baptist: he wanted to prepare the way for faith by focusing on a
person's inner stance, a dimension that cannot easily be expressed:
'all men have a reason, but not all men can give a reason' (*US*, XII, 9).

Existential interiority and the movement of the mind

When most of his contemporaries were trying to find ways to
defend the existence of God using the language of empirical

observation, Newman shifted the focus to what we might call *existential interiority*. As already indicated, his own temperament was highly introspective, perhaps even introverted. But he used this personal characteristic to draw attention to deeper horizons than those explored in the clever apologetics of his colleagues. He insisted again and again that 'faith does not originate in the evidence' people produce, but in something more spontaneous and active, 'more personal and living' (*US*, XI, 5–6). In his view, as he discovered in his brother, the decision for or against faith can often be influenced by unconscious options or assumptions rather than by clear ideas. Each person is swayed by powerful and not always explicit principles and habits, and especially so in matters of religious commitment. Unless we pay attention to the more tacit zones of our reflections, we will be in danger of mistaking our surface explanations for the real operations of our minds.

In a magnificent metaphor Newman evoked the movement of our thinking as similar to an expert mountain climber, who intuitively scales difficult slopes but who cannot explain every step of his adventure to others:

> The mind ranges to and fro, and spreads out, and advances forward with a quickness which has become a proverb, and a subtlety and versatility which baffle investigation. It passes on from point to point … it makes progress not unlike a clamberer on a steep cliff, who, by quick eye, prompt hand, and firm foot, ascends how he knows not himself; by personal endowments and by practice, rather than by rule, leaving no track behind him, and unable to teach another … And such mainly is the way in which all men, gifted or not gifted, commonly reason,—not by rule, but by an inward faculty (*US*, XIII, 7).

Newman's trait of self-reflection was not a matter of lonely subjectivity. Certainly, his approach was psychological and moral (two words he used about his work), but its goal was to arrive at commitment and action. He wanted to do justice to the dynamism of our searching and finding. In this light the much admired cadences of his prose were more than an aesthetic exercise: they seek to embody the subtlety and spontaneous energy of the inquiring mind. One Newman saying, famous enough to be used in the wrapping of the Italian chocolates called Baci, is the following: 'to live is to change, and to be perfect is to have changed often'. It comes from his study of the development of doctrine, a book that coincided with his conversion to Catholicism in 1845. But in fact it was a life-long anchor and characteristic of his thought. At the age of 15 he was captivated by the phrase 'Growth the only evidence of life'. Much later Darwin's theories did not disturb him as they did many of his contemporaries: in a letter of 1874 he commented that there is 'nothing in the theory of evolution inconsistent with an Almighty God.'

Both his celebrated elegance of style and his focus on the drama of development echo Newman's sense of faith as a continuing discovery. For Newman certitude was never static but rather an adventure of deepening. One of his favourite terms was 'enlargement', and he applied it both to education and to the life of the believer. Therefore it is quite unfaithful to his vision to depict him as supporting a mainly doctrinal or immobile theology of faith (as unfortunately is a tendency in certain quarters today). Just as he underlined the involvement of the whole person in arriving at faith, so too he evoked the spiritual 'venture' (another favourite word) of living out one's faith.

The 'realising' role of imagination

Newman's personalism inaugurates a new school of thinking about faith that has many followers in more recent times. As we have seen he seeks to build bridges between the search for religious truth and a person's spiritual and moral qualities, his or her lived dispositions. The focus is not on pure thinking or some separated version of rationality, but on the process of discovering truth and acting on it. This is what is implied by Newman's favourite term 'real'. The opposite of the real is the notional, indicating an intellectualism remote from the drama of decision and commitment. Here Newman was being courageously counter-cultural. He wanted to unmask the illusion of neutrality that had come to captivate his contemporaries (and ours) as the only credible way to truth. In its place, and somewhat in the spirit of St Augustine, he explored the more personal drama of our seeking and finding. His aim was to defend what Lonergan would later call 'authentic subjectivity'.

If Newman had lived a century later, he might well have used the term 'existential' in place of 'real'. It is fascinating that in the drafts of his *Grammar of Assent* he had first written about 'imaginative assent' and only later decided to replace 'imaginative' with 'real'. (In fact he missed a few examples and so the earlier expression is still found in the text). In all probability the reason for the change was an understandable fear of being misunderstood: even today people can easily confuse 'imaginative' with 'imaginary', and therefore faith is seen as a form of fantasy. For Newman, however, the positive role of imagination in faith became a major concern, especially in the years when he was working on his *Grammar of Assent*. For him the function of imagination was literally to 'realise' faith, in the sense of making God real in a person's life.

One of his most forceful statements on imagination comes from 1841 in a series of letters to the newspaper in which he attacked Sir Robert Peel. Opening a new public library at Tamworth, this leading politician had suggested that the fruits of religion could now be acquired through education in literature and science. The idea horrified Newman because it was so contrary not only to his sense of the uniqueness of religious truth, but to his whole anthropology. In reply he expressed his philosophy of the human person as more than a 'reasoning animal', as made for action and moved by feeling. In this context he claimed that 'the heart is commonly reached, not through the reason, but through the imagination' (*GA*, 92). The importance of this insight is underlined by the fact that nearly thirty years later Newman quoted some pages of his diatribe against Peel in the *Grammar of Assent*, and went on to argue that faith needs to be 'discerned, rested in, and appropriated as a reality, by the religious imagination'. (*GA* 98). He added that 'the theology of a religious imagination' gives 'a living hold on truths' and therefore opens the door towards 'habits of personal religion' (*GA*, 117). There is an important pastoral insight here: unless religious truth touches our imagination in some way, it will fail to become personally alive.

Newman also saw imagination as a key battleground for faith. It was a zone of fragility, where surface or distorted images of religion could make unbelief seem plausible or natural. In his notebook he once wrote that 'imagination, not reason, is the great enemy to faith'. But for the most part he saw it as a zone of promise where faith could become spiritually 'real'. He would certainly approve of methods of prayer that visualise scenes of the Gospel in order to make them come alive, but imagination for him is larger than the visual: it points to human sensibility, rather than intellect on its own, as the place where we can best 'discern' and 'appropriate' the realities of faith. In his view we can affirm the statement 'there is a God' on two completely different levels. It can remain a 'cold and ineffective acceptance' when 'imaginations are not at all kindled' and therefore hearts are not inflamed. But that same sentence can work 'a revolution in the mind' whenever it becomes 'held in the imagination' and 'embraced with real assent' (*GA*, 126–127). When imagination awakens, faith escapes from the impersonal and become fruitfully existential. This is an important element in Newman's faith map. Through imagination, rather than through intellectual reflection, we arrive at religious certitude and we open the door to concrete religious commitments. For him imagination is a zone of intuitive logic and as such a key mediator of faith.

From the point of view of more contemporary theologies of faith, Newman's intuitions about imagination seem especially prophetic. Today we speak of healing the divorce between theology and spirituality, or of rethinking the role of the affective and the aesthetic dimensions in faith. When Newman insists that imagination reaches hearts, and makes faith 'real', he is in harmony with these developments. More recent thinkers, ranging from Einstein to Ricoeur, have explored imagination as an essential form of cognition. Newman in his less systematic way had already pointed in this direction. Other writers such as William Lynch or David Tracy have explored the Christian incarnational imagination. For Newman, too, imagination was a vehicle of definiteness, worthy both of the Incarnation and of the drama of religious conversion. In this way imagination is a bridge between the historical definiteness of Incarnation and the more subjective and interior roads that lead us to the yes of faith.

In the voice of Newman (an imaginary monologue)

Most people have heard about my conversion to Catholicism in 1845, and of course that was a pivotal moment in my life. But it was more concerned with church than with faith. I would put my conversion to faith much earlier, in the autumn of 1816 when a period of crisis and breakthrough gave me a new sense of God that lasted for the rest of my life. With my passion for reading I had been flirting with the ideas of some radical atheists, such as Hume, and I found their arguments impressive and plausible. From their external perspective God seemed incredible. For me, with my conventional Christian upbringing, it shook my foundations. I was just fifteen, with all the usual fragilities of adolescence, magnified by a financial crisis in the family that caused me to stay on alone at my boarding school through the summer holidays. In fact I fell sick but, a little like St Ignatius of Loyola, that illness proved a major turning point for me.

It was providential that a young teacher at the school, Rev Walter Mayers, took me under his wing. He was a kindly Evangelical Calvinist and offered me alternative reading, to help me to see the limitations of those empirical thinkers. More importantly, he guided me towards a more personal discovery of God. I experienced, prayerfully and powerfully, that God spoke to me in my conscience and that this God was both real and greater than my individual existence. It was a moment of revelation and of grace that never again left me. It was not simply an emotional or even a sudden conversion: gradually, over a number of months, I arrived at a firm belief in God's mercy and providence, and a definite sense of being called into a lasting relationship with Christ. It was a change of heart, certainly, but also an enlargement of my mind. From reading a book by Thomas Scott, called *The Force of Truth*, I realised that life could be a long love affair with truth, an adventure that demanded total fidelity, and that being faithful to God's truth would mean a constant battle against the more superficial world in me and around me.

Earnestness of attitude

All my life since then I tried to be 'earnest in seeking the truth'.
I used those words in my very first university sermon at the
tender age of 25, and they sum up what I had discovered in
that autumn nearly ten years earlier. It was an insight that I
came back to again and again: it is futile and ultimately
frustrating to discuss religious questions in a detached or
disinterested tone. They can only be approached a certain
personal involvement, recognising the importance of being
earnest! As I liked to say, who would listen to a lecture on
colour by a blind person?

There was another early experience that shaped my
approach to faith, that has to do with a certain quality of
honesty in how we approach faith. Perhaps earnestness was
what I found missing in my younger brother Charles, when I
made the mistake of trying to argue him out of his unbelief. We
debated this in conversations and letters over two years starting in 1823. I came painfully to understand that if a person's
disposition is not open, we lack an essential starting point for
communicating about God. Without a personal desire to seek
the truth and without some element of prayerfulness, the
intellect on its own can become arrogant. Those two youthful
experiences of mine set a seal on my approach to faith.

What seemed missing in my troubled brother (who later
became a militant socialist) I came also to see as lacking in the
culture around me. Later I compared it to someone who sits
complacently at home, as if waiting for God to show up, but
unwilling to make any move towards faith. Having devoted so
much of my life to study and writing, I can hardly be called
anti-intellectual, but I certainly became suspicious of the
intellect when isolated with other dimensions of our humanity. Thus, in my own way, I discovered the truth expressed in
the *Magnificat*, with its evocation of blockages and openings
to faith: proud princes will find themselves scattered in the
imagination of their hearts, but those who hunger humbly will
be filled with good things. Something of the same battle of
dispositions is found in the words of Christ about revelation

being hidden from the learned and clever but available to children (Matt. 11.25).

Starting from within

So, what would I suggest to faith searchers of today? First of all, there is a choice of wavelength to be made: you can approach the question of God 'notionally' or with your full humanity. If you are not in touch with the movements of your inner self, it will be hard to reach any sense of God being 'real'. Because it is a relational truth, not one discovered through a merely objective stance. The quality of your presence to the question is crucial. Whatever answer you arrive at will transform how you see everything. And you need to be involved in the search because, if it is a genuine search, you will be changed by the answer.

If your disposition is not open, honest and receptive, you are already blocking the path, perhaps without knowing it. When I ask you to listen to your heart or conscience, it is not an invitation to sentimental escapism. What you need to escape from is a narrow or impersonal rationalism. Perhaps our universities have been kidnapped, for a century of more now, by an idol of verifiable objectivity that can never do justice to the full stretch of our wonder. It throws in the sponge over being able to answer our larger questions. None of the great existential issues of life can be faced in this impersonal way. Whenever knowledge is more than factual, your freedom is involved. It is like the human adventure of falling in love, or of being-in-love. To say 'yes' to someone involves a certain risk. It is a decision to trust that goes beyond the external evidence. So our important experiences are never just external. We experience every day the strange inner adventure of our attitudes and feelings, of our sensibility and our hopes, even if outer realities seem to monopolise and even kidnap our attention.

It is not easy to do justice to the delicate convergence of elements needed for religious belief. Faith is not born from reasoning in the narrow sense, and yet it is profoundly reasonable. It does not reject the intellect but it needs a certain quality of inquiry that broadens out to embrace dimensions of yourself that do not lend themselves to easy explanation or expression. Faith, I so often said, appeals to the heart, and yet that does not mean it is merely a question of feeling. Faith is rooted in your experience of conscience, and yet it is not simply a matter of morality. Faith, we insist, is free. It is a truth to be embraced as a decision, and yet it is more than a leap into the dark, an impulsive surrender.

Conscience as presence

In various moments of my life I stressed different dimensions of our faith adventure. From youth to old age, a central strand of my faith lay in the experience of conscience and this was always more important for me than outer avenues of verification. Perhaps I captured this best in my novel, *Callista*, published in 1855, which tells the story of a sophisticated Greek girl living in North Africa in the third century and of her gradual discovery of Christian faith. At one stage when Callista has become aware of her 'inner Guide' but has not yet encountered the Word of the Gospel, she has a conversation with a pagan philosopher who believes only in an 'eternal self-existing something'. This is too vague for Callista, who tells him that she experiences a more concrete sense of God in her conscience.

> I feel myself in His presence. He says to me, 'Do this; don't do that' ... it is the echo of a person speaking to me ... I believe in what is more than a mere 'something.' I believe in what is more real to me than sun, moon, stars, and the fair earth, and the voice of friends. You will say, Who is He? Has He ever told you anything about Himself? Alas! no! – the more's the pity. But I will not give up what I have, because I have not more. An echo implies a voice; a voice a speaker. That speaker I love and I fear. (*C*, 314–315)

I repeated that image of an imperative 'echo of a voice' in other writings of mine. It points to a threshold between natural and revealed religion. I always had deep respect for conscience as the core and climax of natural religion and as preparing people for the Word of revelation. In fact this inner presence, even when not fully recognised, is the way most people in history have encountered God. It is where God is present to people without their knowing it clearly, and where their desire is kept alive for a more explicit revelation. In the twenty-first century not many people resonate with my acute sense of conscience. Believers today rarely share my experience of a commanding, and even fearful, inner voice. Perhaps there was sometimes too much guilt in my religion, but something precious is lost when we forget how to listen to our conscience. If sin loses its seriousness then, in my view, religion has become too human and too soft.

Even today I would want to invite you to become aware of the movements of that inner voice, and to allow it to guide you towards God. Think about it this way. In your actual living you try to be faithful to certain values or absolutes even though you may not like that word. Without necessarily naming them, you live from certain fundamental options. These are the non-negotiable anchors and goals of your life. There are certain things that you would not do for 'love or money', because they would contradict or even destroy your very identity. If so, that is 'conscience' or fidelity to a light that you follow – like those ancient Magi. It is here that you grow, in ways that you cannot measure, towards 'living no longer for yourself' as St Paul says (2 Cor. 5.15).

Grasping the real

In later life, as I worked for years on my book *The Grammar of Assent*, I came to highlight two other dimensions of our road to faith: imagination and what I called the 'illative sense'. Just as in my early days, I was put off by impersonal and complicated arguments about the existence of God, now I realised that without my imagination being awakened, God can never become 'real' to the heart. Religion can easily remain 'notional', like those people described by Jesus as praying 'Lord, Lord' but never arriving at a change in their actions. This is the distinction between what I called nominal and 'vital' Christianity. I think that most people who try to pray have experienced the huge difference between drifting around in ideas and being really touched by the Spirit.

The word 'illative' points in the same direction of becoming-real. It comes from Latin, implying grasping an issue. It is an important capacity that we use every day to recognise truth. It is our ability to say 'yes' and to feel sure about it. We make judgements all the time, instinctively understanding when a convergence of evidence allows us to affirm something as true. We know that we know, even though we cannot explain all the steps. We grasp things intuitively and arrive at security in our knowing. And on that basis in daily life we take a stance. We are able to commit ourselves and act. Yes, 'we need something higher than a mere balance of arguments'. We need 'a real hold and habitual intuition of the objects of Revelation' (*GA*, 238).

In brief, what am I saying? Look inward rather than outward. Pay attention to your conscience. Nourish your imagination. Trust your living mind and its capacity to reach truth. In short, the roads that lead us to faith are more ordinary than we think, but our ideas and our life-styles may have robbed us of essential anchors. We lack inner quiet. Our wonder suffers from malnutrition. Our picture of truth can be restricted to the externally provable. Our image of our searching can be that of the lone cowboy riding into the desert. But our humanity calls out for other kinds of food. It has deeper hungers and questions, which can be suppressed or neglected in the dominant model of life. There is another kind of knowledge, equally certain but more strange in its wavelength. It involves the mind, the heart, the spirit, the whole self. It needs another starting point within us, a different quality of seeking. We also have to journey out of ourselves, humbly wondering, and then perhaps we can encounter and be surprised by a different Word.

Much of this is about being ready. 'The readiness is all', said Shakespeare in the mouth of Hamlet. The process of our knowing about God is not really different from the processes we use every day to arrive at certainties that we live (without argument, analysis, or working it all out logically). What is different in religious faith is not the road towards it, but the vision of life revealed in God's self-giving. But *how* we arrive there is through ordinary fidelity to who we are – when we are fully ourselves. *What* we learn from God is extraordinary – a surprise that can slowly transform our lives. And that is another story.

References to works of John Henry Newman

A   *Apologia pro Vita Sua*, London, 1908.
C   *Callista: A Tale of the Third Century*, London, 1928.
GA   *An Essay in Aid of a Grammar of Assent*, London, 1909.
LD   *Letters and Diaries*, Vol. I, ed. I. Ker & T. Gornall, Oxford, 1978.
PPS   *Parochial and Plain Sermons*, Vol. I, London, 1907.
US   *Fifteen Sermons Preached before the University of Oxford*, London, 1909. (References to these university sermons give the number of the sermon in Roman numerals and then the number of the paragraph rather than the page number.)

2

Maurice Blondel: the theatre of desire

In many underground stations in London the traveller is greeted with a recorded voice repeating 'mind the gap'. It could be an entry point for Blondel's philosophy. He invites us to become aware of a perpetual sense of self-dissatisfaction because our best desires are never fully realised in our actions. Again and again we fall short of what Shakespeare's Cleopatra calls our 'immortal longings'. By recognising that gap we can begin to sense our need for God.

> Yes or no, has life a meaning, and do human beings have a destiny? I act without knowing what action is, without having wished to live, without really knowing who I am ... I seem condemned to life, condemned to death, condemned to eternity! Why and by what right, if I have neither known it or willed it? (*A*, 3).

A daring thesis

With these anguished questions, Blondel introduced his doctoral dissertation of 1893 and set a whole new tone for philosophy. Instead of a conventionally scholarly style, this young French student dared to evoke the inner drama of existence. The courage to take this approach came from his own religious faith and spiritual life. Twelve years earlier, he had arrived in Paris to study philosophy, hoping to share his Christian vision with his university companions. But he ran into a brick wall of disinterest and even of disdain for the very question of God. He found himself confronted, as Pascal before him, with an intellectual world incapable of delving into the real issues because caught in 'the negations of rationalism' (*LA*, 134). Gradually he chose to become a philosophical John the Baptist, preparing the way for revelation. To invite people to reflect on the possibility of God, as a reality hidden within their own action, became the passion of his life.

Newman and Blondel both represent an important shift in thinking about faith – away from thinking about truth-on-its-own to discovering a more living truth through the exercise of our freedom. Where Newman stressed the 'real' as opposed to the 'notional', Blondel explored human action as the key to the drama of human existence. If it was a risk to voice existential struggles in an academic thesis, more daring still was Blondel's enlarging of the debate by pointing to Christianity as a source of healing. Through reflecting on who we are and what we do, he saw us coming up against a fundamental choice: either we remain locked in self-sufficiency or else we move towards religious faith.

In this zone of our freedom, he argued, we can discover that God is already active as the artist of all our searching. But first, we need to experience that gap or contradiction in our desires: on the one hand we 'do all we can, as if we had only ourselves to depend on', on the other we have to admit that 'all we do … is radically insufficient' (*A*, 354). Thus we run into an incurable incompleteness in our yearning: 'it is true to its infinite ambition only inasmuch as it recognizes its infinite powerlessness' (*A*, 345–6). We come up against the basic fact that what is indispensable for a full life appears inaccessible – at least if we rely on ourselves alone. And so the possibility of God enters the scene as 'absolutely impossible and absolutely necessary' (*A*, 357). What begins as a painful gap can open the path to faith as a perfect fit for the human condition, if and when the 'supernatural' meets the cry of our human nature.

A purifying exodus

To recognise one's fundamental lack of fulfilment involves changing perspective. If someone is living on the surface, it means stopping being a mere spectator of one's activities to become aware of that painful distance between hopes and achievements. But not many people 'have interest in anything lacking!' (*A*, 333). They are not aware of 'the most profound drama of the interior life' (*A*, 330). What Blondel calls his 'method of immanence' is a way of paying attention to these contradictions and of coming to recognise our innermost needs (cf. *LA*, 157). He was blunt about the purification required in order to arrive at an integrated 'life of action'. In order to let God take first place in one's existence, a person's own preferences have to give way: what you do not kill in yourself, can kill you, because your self-will can keep you from living your own true desire (cf. *A*, 345).

Although he does not quote the Gospel that 'without me you can do nothing', a key conversion comes, according to Blondel, when we admit that left to our own devices we are incapable of fulfilling our hopes. This is the paradox of the human condition as Blondel presents it. A confession of impotence becomes a springboard towards a greater freedom. We can then move from acting without a compass to a moment of decision, but not without tears, as older books on language learning used to say. In a culture that has become spiritually soft, the emphasis on 'mortification' can come as a salutary reminder of what Newman had called 'the darker side of religion'. We are faced with two roads. One possibility is to stay embedded in self-sufficiency: 'you will not go out of yourself' (*A*, 340). The second involves an openness to change, entailing 'a death passing on to life' or 'dying that we must live' (*A*, 346, 349). In scriptural terms he is close to St Paul's core transformation from self-effort to trust (Phil. 3:9).

Awakening to sickness

Some of Blondel's keywords are no longer in vogue today: sacrifice, duty, detachment, renunciation, suffering. His theme is what he (like Newman) calls 'disposition' – the zone where we become ready for God, a movement that is seldom possible without disturbing our complacency. We need a healthy and 'incurable discomfort' with the world, making us realise that we are never what we truly want to be (*A*, 350–1). Only if we face this 'supreme human sickness' can we 'succeed in asking the right question' (*LA*, 154).

Who needs this rude awakening? Everyone; but especially those whom Kierkegaard would call 'aesthetic' individuals or whom Lonergan would call drifters. In unusually strong language, Blondel says that a sophisticated avoidance of issues can 'spit upon life' by sacrificing everything to egoism (*A*, 33). Over a century ago he alerted people to the traps of what today is called a 'feel-good' culture: 'if we do only what charms us or what seems advantageous to us' (*A*, 347) we are probably avoiding a deeper call. Thus he pushes us to be less innocent about our battle-grounds.

Once he has established this philosophy of insufficiency as a path to inner freedom, a gentler tone enters: 'How little is required to find access to life!' (*A*, 354). A small act of generosity can open the door to the divine. He expresses this movement of self-transcendence imaginatively: 'a surge of the heart is perhaps enough to ... envelop the infinite' (*A*, 356). In other words, when we find ourselves to be flawed and insufficient, and yet capable of self-giving, we approach a threshold of religious meaning. Is there another Word speaking to us, a possibly different Love reaching out to us, healing our lack of completion? God 'can give Himself only where room is made for Him' (356).

Allies of God

As *L'Action* progresses, Blondel becomes more explicitly religious in his explorations. The quality of our desire becomes central: through reflecting on our deepest longings we recognise them as gifts from God. Indeed 'the great effort of the heart is to believe in God's love'. It is at this crossroads between unfulfilled desire and gift that philosophy opens up to revelation. It is here that we know our need of a saviour who will be 'the act of our acts, the prayer of our prayer' (*A*, 366-7). It is here that God's action enters and we receive what we can never achieve. Then our action becomes 'coextensive with that of God' (*LA*, 200).

By taking human action as his focus, Blondel moves away from any philosophy forgetful of the drama of human existence. For him faith becomes reality only through practical living. 'It is through the channel of action that revealed truth penetrates deep into thought' (*A*, 368). His advice to unbelievers is to 'take the decisive step of action', because faith is reached, not reached by an effort of thought, but by concrete generosity. And because God is at work in this self-giving, we 'enter into a new world where no philosophical speculation' could lead us (*A*, 371).

The argument advances towards spiritual claims that must have shocked his examiners, accustomed as they were to a more academic discourse. By faith and love, according to Blondel, we

participate in the life of God, becoming by grace what God is by
nature. Our human zones of choice and commitment become our
'way of thinking and praying', where the slow process of converting
our desires 'engenders God' in us. The movement of our freedom
invites us to 'ally' ourselves with God and in this light faith can be
'called the divine experience within us' (*A*, 378–9).

Struggle, consolation, fruitfulness

One of the most frequent accusations against religious belief is that
it makes no earthly difference. For Blondel this would be a serious
charge if it were true. If a believer is not living some process of
ego-erosion and of service to others, then his or her faith is not
genuine. Through our life-styles and concrete options we make
faith real and make its truth shine. It is a truth that is never grasped
by the mind alone, but only by the mind in harmony with certain
dispositions of the heart and decisions of the will.

Once again we come back to a recurring theme of these chapters
– that the recognition of God that we call faith is not the same as
affirming the existence of a First Cause for the universe. Faith is a
relational response to a Word of Love, and this response is always
more than an intellectual affair. It is marked by movement into the
unknown: 'Wherever we stop, God is not; wherever we walk
forward, God is, [but] always beyond' (*A*, 325). It is an adventure of
the whole person with the changing contexts of life. And if it is
authentic faith, it will embody itself in practices that are resist and
challenge the dominant culture. As Jesus said, his disciples will
recognisable by their love.

However, if we over-stress the struggle and the differentness of
faith, we are in danger of forgetting its consolation and its fulfilling
fruitfulness. In Blondel's words, in our self-sufficiency 'we wanted
to do everything by ourselves', but once we embrace the Christian
road, God acts within us leading us towards a 'perfect synthesis' (*A*,
388). Union takes over from tension. What God wants of us
coincides, in a surprising way, with what we most deeply desire. We
share in God's freedom and even in God's loving. Such graced
companionship can sometimes be experienced in the life of a
believer, and when this consolation comes, we know without expla-

nations that this is the true music of existence. Here we can feel, as one of the Gospel parables says, the joy of discovering the treasure hidden in the field of life.

Knowing through love

For his day Blondel is surprisingly and prophetically positive about unbelievers. He satirises those who evade the religious question, but he has a generous sense of 'the invisible kingdom of grace' (*LA*, 195) at work in those who cannot arrive at faith. In this he is a precursor of Rahner and, indeed, of most theologians today. In Blondel's words 'souls of good will' can nevertheless become 'in an invisible way, and in their heart of hearts, sharers in what they are not aware of possessing' (*LA*, 193). This is because 'God's secret summons' is present in their choices and actions (*LA*, 141). Revelation 'seeks us out, so to speak, on our own ground and pursues us into our inner fastnesses' (*LA*, 155). Blondel's strategy, as already seen, is to stimulate hope for faith, by his rereading of the theatre of desire and action. He trusts that people may one day recognise the inner drama of their existence, because within their self-imposed isolation lies a longing for something more, or for Someone more.

On Whitsunday 1961 Dag Hammarskjöld, then Secretary General of the United Nations, wrote in his spiritual diary (later published as *Markings*): 'at some moment I did answer Yes to Someone – or Something – and from that hour I was certain that existence is meaningful and that, therefore, my life, in self-surrender, had a goal.' Maurice Blondel would relish that sentence. Indeed, the final page of his thesis speaks of a spiritual experience that cannot be demonstrated by reason: 'before this *yes* without any *no*, and here alone, all is decided absolutely' (*A*, 446). Both writers point to a zone of openness and option where the quality of a life is shaped.

Blondel can be seen as a cross between Pascal, Kierkegaard and Meister Eckhart. With Pascal he shares an impatience with surface living and shallow thinking: refusal to choose is still a choice, but an irresponsible one. Like Kierkegaard his tone is urgent because so much is at stake: we cannot be truly ourselves by ourselves. Like Eckhart (whom he never mentions) he want to reveal the spiritual unity that is possible for people: 'help us move from a life that is divided to a life that is one' (Eckhart).

Late in life, when he was about 85, Blondel found an attractive image to capture the core of his thought. He recalled that the dome of Pantheon in Rome has no keystone to hold it together. Instead there is an opening to the sky, through which light comes into the huge edifice. In similar fashion our spiritual journey reaches up, like an unfinished building, to a gap through which divine light can shine. Thus the experience of incompleteness becomes positive because it can put us, again and again, in touch with the language of faith. To become aware of our dissatisfaction with the finite is a pointer towards the infinite. Beyond the fragility and emptiness another possibility awaits. Underlying all our conscious desires and actions, which swing inevitably between egoism and self-giving, Blondel leads us to recognise a Greater Desire hidden within us, placed there by God, where God is present to us. Philosophy can bring us only to this threshold of faith. It points to a deeper hunger and a deeper possibility. To cross that threshold is to discover living truth, living freedom and a different source of joy.

In the final words of Blondel's great work, he deliberately goes beyond philosophy to comment on the *yes* of his own Christian faith: it is a certitude, which 'cannot be communicated, because it arises only from the intimacy of totally personal action' (*A*, 446). He had diagnosed the contradictions of action without a goal, had discerned its implicit quest for a meaning beyond the visible, had confronted the cost of being faithful to that dynamism, and now finally he arrives at a condition of simplicity. He is able to name the Gift that crowns his journey and without which that Gift cannot be recognised: 'we know nothing if we do not love' (*A*, 406). After a long road of reflection, we encounter a paradoxical surprise: the Gift that we discover at the end had been guiding our seeking from the start.

In the voice of Blondel (*an imaginary monologue/meditation*)

Whether we like it or not, we are thrown into a world of action. This does not mean that life is like an 'action movie', full of dramatic episodes. But it does mean that I cannot avoid 'doing'. I get up in the morning. I do all sorts of things during the day. Ever since I stopped being an infant, I entered a world of tasks and commitments, with more or less liberty of choice. I suspect that most of the time my level of conscious freedom is not very high. But each day is filled with action.

Beyond a fragmented life

Sooner or later the question arises, quietly but insistently: does any of this make sense? Has it a purpose, or is it just a chaotic accumulation of events? I didn't ask to be born. I found myself within this family. Later on, I may not have had much of a role in deciding my life situation, even my work. A lot of existence seems fated, not fully chosen by me. Why does it so often seem a routine road? Where in this desert of the everyday is the great adventure of my humanity?

They tell me that my existence is precious, that it could have eternal significance. They tell me stories of meaning, or stories that try to give a shape to things. But the concrete realities of my life don't seem to support such metaphysical vistas. I act, without setting the compass of my freedom. I act, day in day out, in ways that make little or no sense to me. My deeds seem random, fragmented and unfocused. And yet this is my clearest certainty: I exist and I act, but a painful distance separates my realities from my hopes.

There is movement, yes, but it can seem like a river meandering in search of the sea, or even like a dog chasing its tail. Is it purposeful, in a hidden way, or futile, no matter how hard one seeks? Everyone makes choices, but have they any unity? Everything seems shadowed by compromise or by practicality. It adds up to an unrooted life. And so a disturbing question comes: is it all up to me? Am I ultimately alone with these bits and pieces of existence, like a jig-saw with no final solution?

Glimpsing another possibility

If I get frightened, and throw in the sponge, I have accepted a life of drifting, or at best, an existence like a lighthouse, sometimes with flashes of light, but without them most of the time. And what if the light flashing is only the product of my longing for some light? If so, I am thrown back into the prison of self. But what if, within the adventure of my small freedom, there are pointers to a greater, even an infinite, freedom? What if my shy hope for 'something more' is not just a fleeting illusion? What if all this lack of fulfilment is a call to raise my sights? If I honestly admit that something is missing in my life, I might be able to listen to a promise beyond the immediacy of each day. And if that call came from God, my existence, so shadowed by failure, could be healed into hope.

How might this happen, this transformation from frustration to trust? A first step is when I stop merely doing and become conscious of my core self. Remember so many saints who experienced new grace when forced to slow down by sickness: Ignatius discovering the inner battleground in his sickbed in Loyola, or Newman with his own version of new awareness when unwell at 15 years of age. There are moments of self-awakening and even of self-joy. Then I become present to myself, only to discover that I do not belong to myself alone. Where all seemed doomed to incompleteness, now it moves towards unity, towards more than I can imagine or understand. The old sense of self-contradiction disappears when I am drawn beyond myself by a magnet or Presence that can only be called Love. I come to recognise a Presence that was active within my action all the time.

A crossroads of decision

If I wake up to option, seeing that the quality of my life lies in my hands, that discovery is both exciting and frightening. Drifting half-consciously through each day becomes unworthy of who I am and who I can be. But it is too simple to say that I am now in control of my destiny. That delusion will not last for long. Living faithful to the light is short-lived, if I am trying to do so on my own resources. So I experience both possibility and impotence together. Again I stand at a crossroads of decision. I need a saviour, with me and within me.

Otherwise I am condemned to a stop-go existence of fits and
starts, and ultimate disappointment.

Behind all my scattered life lies a longing that I ignored
because I had no language for it. I was longing for God, for
infinity, for an eternal love, not as an escape from the finite, but
as a promise making sense of all I do. The lonely achiever
becomes the receiver who is not alone. The faith map
becomes clearer. Start from yourself. Be present to yourself.
Admit the self-disappointment and wait for the birth of a new
hope born from humility. Paradoxically, if you descend, you
can recognise and ascend. First you have to bother to be free,
and then you may realise in a logic of the heart, that, in
Thérèse of Lisieux's famous words, 'all is gift'.

Many familiar expectations are overturned in this approach.
Restlessness is no longer negative. It becomes a gateway to a
promise that calls us forward. We are right to be dissatisfied
with our small selves, in order to get in touch with our hunger
and the Love-Answer to it. But beware: it is not resting that
answers our restlessness, but movement. Just as music exists
only in an unfolding of sound, God does not exist for us except
as moving out of our reach, never captured even in our best
words. Whenever we want to slow down the river of our
wonder, we fall back into mere thoughts, words, images, but
the faith story is always on the move, a continuing exodus. It
becomes a shared adventure: acting with and within God, and
finding that God acts with and within us.

A hidden fire

D. H. Lawrence used to say that that we are blocked by our
smaller desires from getting in touch with our greater desires.
A whole life-style can be addicted to mini-desires, mini-
actions, mini-horizons, and yet smothered beneath all this
busy-ness lurks a larger hope for fullness, for eternity, for God.
Perhaps those mini-desires can even be self-giving and good,
but they are not enough. They are not the whole story. They do
not fully satisfy the heart – as St Augustine knew with pain and

expressed so eloquently: 'there I was going mad on the road to sanity'.

A moment of grace can arrive when the ancient words of Psalm 61 take fire and come alive. 'My soul is longing for you like a dry weary land without water'. From underneath all the fragmented living, a core desire is released from its hiding place. It is like a fire that burns away all that is secondary and that lights the path towards salvation. Just as in Ezechiel's famous image, an experience of freshness takes away the heart of stone and puts me in touch with the heart of flesh.

The daily struggle

In short, I stand at a daily crossroads, caught between two conflicting images. One is of holding my life, defensively and alone, in my own hands – the illusion of self-mastery. But another possibility enters if my imagination opens, suddenly or slowly, to a pledge of companionship. Here relationship replaces self-will. The initiative is no longer mine but Another's. To repeat: either I continue on my own, or I recognise Someone as already creatively and lovingly guiding my actions. The hunger for God – as Saviour – is born when I admit defeat, and my story stops being soliloquy.

All of this can seem too smooth a plan. The full story is never so straightforward. There will be a daily pendulum of moods. But along that unsteady road of each day the heart's focus is tested and nourished. Even here there can be moments when, like the character Henderson in Saul Bellow's novel, I hear a voice inside me crying 'I want, I want', even though frustratingly it never finishes the sentence. Through this voice of restless desire I can realise that I am not fully at home where I am. I am 'living and partly living' (T. S. Eliot). Once more I am confronted by the 'supreme alternative' (Blondel): either my desiring turns in on myself, like Narcissus, or else I open to a love story where I gradually learn to belong to Another.

In this respect an attractive parallel to Blondel can be found in one of George Herbert's poems of three centuries earlier. The title offers an image not repeated in the text itself: 'The Pulley'. God is pictured as operating a pulley, whereby what weighs us down paradoxically raises us up. The poem imagines the Creator as having a 'glass of blessings' and pouring them out one by one on humanity – beauty, wisdom, pleasure and so on.

> When almost all was out, God may a stay,
> Perceiving that alone of all his treasure
> Rest in the bottom lay.

If God were to give us complete repose in this life, we could 'rest' there and not seek any further. So the final verse, with a typical pun, shows the pulley of restlessness hoisting us towards faith:

> Yet let him keep the rest,
> But keep them with repining restlessness:
> Let him be rich and weary, that at least,
> If goodness lead him not, yet weariness
> May toss him to my breast.

References to works of Maurice Blondel

A   *Action (1893): Essay on a Critique of Life and a Science of Practice*, Notre Dame IN, 1984.

LA   *Letter on Apologetics and History of Dogma*, ed. and trans. A. Dru and I. Trethowan, London, 1964.

3

Karl Rahner: the magnetism of mystery

Karl Rahner is often looked on as the most important Catholic theologian of the twentieth century, greatly admired by some, while severely criticised by others. Why such deep divisions about him? It seems a question of two different mentalities. For those conscious of a changed and complex culture around us and of the need for different languages of faith, Rahner is seen as a figure of spiritual and intellectual courage. Even his major critic, Hans Urs von Balthasar, recognised a genuine pastoral urgency in Rahner's desire to make sense of faith for post-war Europe. Not all of Rahner's critics are so generous: some see him as the source of many of the ills of today's Church. Usually, these opponents of his belong to what Lonergan calls the 'classicist' model of theology, which stresses what is permanent and universal, and remains suspicious of starting points that seem too 'anthropological'.

Certainly, Rahner gave pride of place to each person's hidden encounter with the Spirit of God, insisting, like Newman, that this subjective approach was not in danger of falling into mere subjectivism, because, ultimately, God's grace is universal and the source of all our self-transcendence. In his words 'the most objective reality of salvation is at the same time necessarily the most subjective: the direct relationship with God' (*TI*, IX, 36). A constant refrain of Rahner's work is that everyone is in contact with God's action, whether they recognise it or not. Being intensely aware of a new moment of history, when faith seemed to have lost touch with human experience, he wanted to re-build the bridges between inner depth and the Christian vision.

Of course, as many have remarked, his style was over-complex, at times convoluted and marked by heavy philosophical jargon. There is a well-known story of his older brother, Hugo, also a Jesuit, saying that he would dedicate his old age to translating Karl into German! But these communication difficulties are not the main problem. Now, a quarter of a century after his death, the question is whether Rahner was perhaps too much a man of his own generation. Trying to meet the challenges of secular modernity, he gave prominence to the meaning-adventure of individuals – possibly at the expense of a social dimension in theology. He has also been criticised for neglecting more traditional expressions and supports of faith, such as sacraments, church belonging, the details of biblical revelation, or the doctrinal content of catechesis. This chapter will seek to highlight what seems permanently valuable in his work. One thing is certain: rooted in a profound knowledge of the Catholic tradition, he tried passionately to outline a deeper map of faith to meet the needs of he called a 'winter season'.

Collapse of a culture

Where does one begin to enter the huge world of Rahner? Since our focus is on faith, perhaps the best entry point is his sense of a crisis of religious belief in his lifetime. What had changed, he insisted, was not so much faith as the context for a decision of faith. Probably no other major theologian has devoted so much sympathetic attention to atheism and agnosticism. He was also acutely aware that the language of preaching and church teaching often rang hollow for believers themselves, and that merely repeating Christian truths in old formulas had become pastorally futile. In a pre-modern culture the Church and its traditions of worship seemed to be automatically at the centre of life. But now people swim in a different cultural ocean, live with more questions and complexity, and have often lost contact with any inner experience of faith. And therefore religious customs, which suited a village context, now appear remote, tired, and incapable of nourishing the spirit. If such traditional expressions of religion have collapsed, according to Rahner faith needs to be fostered in much more personal ways.

Once Rahner sensed that a whole language of faith was dying, he was driven to look for a more existential faith map. Talking about God in a merely doctrinal or 'propositional' sense was out of touch with what he sensed to be the hungers and needs of the age. It was not a question of watering down faith (as he has sometimes been accused of doing) but of doing justice to possible journeys of faith in a new moment of culture. That meant making each person's inner adventure a key for making sense of God. Rahner's approach focuses less on explicit revelation and more on awakening people to a hidden revelation happening in their everyday depths. It would be 'anthropological' in the sense of starting 'from below', but without ever making the human a measure for the divine. His work is theological and faith-rooted, because he always interpreted this human scene 'from above', reading it as the theatre of God's grace.

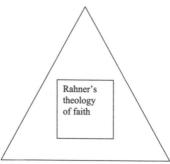

God's universal will to save:
Grace as self-communication of love

Rahner's
theology
of faith

Human self-transcendence: Revelation in history:
openness and orientation to Mystery   explicit Christian faith

Although Rahner's vision can sound complex, it rests on relatively simple foundations, as can be suggested through the image of a triangle. The top of the diagram starts from God's universal will to save all of humanity and hence the reality of transforming grace offered to every person. In this sense Rahner often speaks of the self-communication of God's mystery and love. The downward flow of the right-hand side of the triangle indicates the traditional understanding of Biblical revelation as the source of Christian faith. This is the zone that Rahner calls 'categorical', where explicit faith is born from preaching, sacraments, catechesis and Church belonging. The left-hand side highlights a real but less visible history of salvation, the theatre of the Spirit at work in all people and cultures, prior to any awareness or recognition of the outer Word of revelation. Here we can place Rahner's exploration of our self-transcendence, as an already graced openness to God's call. It is here that God's action reaches us even in hidden ways, which he calls 'unthematic' or 'transcendental'. It is here that an implicit kind of faith becomes possible when people respond to the often unrecognised promptings of the Spirit. The descending line on the right side has been the main avenue of faith through the centuries. For a time of pluralism and secularisation, Rahner wanted to draw attention to another avenue of responding to God's self-giving. The right side remains the privileged road to faith, but the left side is where countless numbers of people are touched by grace without fully knowing it.

Unvisited personal interiority

Rahner's starting point was the gift of God already at work within the human spirit, but his hope was to move from that drama of humanity towards the surprise of Christ, starting so to speak from the left of the diagram and moving towards the right. He believed in a God-given magnetism present in every heart, drawing each person out of themselves towards truth and love. He understood this inner dynamism not just as preparation for God but as God's presence in us. Just as we speak of depth psychology, Rahner was trying to develop a depth theology, starting from human interiority and desire rather than from doctrine or teaching about the Gospel. He believed that God's Spirit is always already there before our preaching, and so it seemed vital to help people to get in touch with their deep and silent experiences of God.

In this light he suggested a new set of preambles for faith. Where the preambles of an older apologetics involved external reasoning towards God's possible existence, these new preambles were spiritual, because God can be discovered at the core of each person's adventure of life. They are intended both for unbelievers and for struggling modern believers willing to undertake some spiritual self-reflection. His starting point for both groups lies more in their experience of questing and questioning than in any mere 'information' about God from beyond. This focus on existential interiority, as found also in Newman, can come as a surprise to people more used to explicit God-talk or more traditional communication of faith. Rahner's preference for this approach is rooted in two fundamental intuitions. On the one hand, many people today live at a

distance from their own depths, and hence overcoming this spiritual malnutrition is a necessary first step. Secondly, as mentioned
already, in these often unvisited personal depths God's Spirit is
already at work, and so there are fruits of that action waiting to be
recognised.

How might one recognise these fruits? By moments when the
person goes beyond his or her self towards truth or love, for
instance by a generosity of service, or a courage in the face of
difficulties, that could never be explained by enlightened self-
interest. These lived expressions of self-transcendence are the fruits
of the Spirit that St Paul lists in the letter to the Galatians (chapter
5). They can be present and alive in people who never think about
God, or darken the doors of churches. Rahner reached back to a
Christian formation process of the first millennium to find a word
for this new apologetics. He called it 'mystagogy', an ancient term
used to describe the journey of preparation for adult baptism – as a
gradual introduction into the mysteries of faith. He wanted to
suggest ways of initiating people of today into the mystery of God
at the centre of their own human mystery. In this sense he spoke of
theology as having self-experience as its starting point. In an
important lecture of 1966 he expressed this core of his thinking:
'there is an experience of grace and this is the real, fundamental
reality of Christianity' (*TI*, IX, 41). In fact, as early as 1954 he had
spoken of 'an uncovering of that Christianity which God in his
grace has already hidden in the hearts of those who think they are
not Christians' (*TI*, III, 371). As late as 1982 he insisted that 'a
mystagogy into this original, grace-filled religious experience is
today of fundamental importance' (*KRD*, 328).

The hidden fruits of grace

Here we are close to his famous or infamous theory of the 'anonymous Christian', an unfortunate expression that Rahner was later
willing to abandon because it left itself open to so many misinter-
pretations. In fact, six years after the theologian's death, Pope John
Paul II, in his encyclical *Redemptoris Missio* (# 10), strongly
affirmed the reality of universal grace and salvation and developed
it in words that echo the essentials of Rahner's vision. He stated

that since salvation 'is offered to all, it must be made concretely available to all', including those who have no opportunity to know the Gospel. The Pope went on to say that 'in a manner known to God', the Spirit offers this possibility to everyone through 'grace secretly at work' in their hearts. Rahner must have been delighted to read this endorsement of a presence of grace active in everyone. This was the reality that he sought to identify and evoke in people's self-experience. In more unified cultures preachers could go straight to the message of the Gospel. But today people have heard the Christian story, or half-heard it, and are often left bored by what seems so familiar. Faced with situations of atheism and increasing distance from Church forms of belonging, Rahner stressed the possibility of a more hidden story of salvation which may or may not arrive at explicit Christian faith.

Needless to say, he saw faith as reaching its completion in Christ. However before we come to acknowledge explicitly that climax of revelation, each one of us is in graced and living contact with invisible mystery. In this light he advocated a more indirect ministry of faith, aiming to bring people to awareness of the grace they already encounter and may already live. In order to communicate this different approach he suggested that something of the wavelength of poetry is needed. Much preaching uses predictable language that fails to put people in contact with their deep self-experience of grace. Instead Rahner's proposal of 'mystagogy' has been described as a catechism of the heart. Rahner would surely agree with Newman's famous statement about reaching the heart through the imagination, adding perhaps that an imaginative faith-map for today should evoke the grace quietly at work in each person. In his view it is often along that interior and spiritual route that people will discover God now. In terms of the earlier diagram, this 'shift of emphasis in our proclamation' (*TI*, XXI, 150) could be located at the base of the triangle, as the line that moves from left to right. Rahner started from attention to the 'experience of transcendence' (*FCF*, 59) in the hope of moving towards the fullness of Christian faith.

But such a spiritual road is not easy to travel, as Rahner was well aware. He pictured us as victims of a frenetic life-style that allows little room either for poetic wonder or for recognising the struggle of our lived attitudes (here there are echoes of Blondel). For Rahner, everything we do is an expression of a yes or a no to love. It is here in this battleground of the heart that the Spirit draws us towards faith and towards losing our small ego in the vastness of God. To adapt one of Rahner's metaphors, this orientation of human existence towards God is like a river seeking the ocean. Just as a river will wind its way through different landscapes, but always unconsciously drawn towards the sea, so our self-transcendence carries us, often unaware, towards the ultimate horizon that is God. 'Faith is hopeful faith, else it would not be faith' (*KRD*, 89).

Rahner often comes back to a distinction between what he calls 'transcendental' and 'categorical', which can be translated as what we live implicitly and what we express explicitly. We can live an option for generous love without putting it into words or without openly recognising its source in God's grace. We can also, tragically, live a closure to love without seeing that in this way we contradict the gift of God within us. More than other religious thinkers, and certainly more than in previous theology, Rahner gives priority to these silent, unconscious dimensions of existence. The hope of God is that we would come to know Christ explicitly, but since this is culturally impossible for many people, there has to be another road: a faith lived without knowing itself explicitly, without putting itself into words, and without living a conscious relationship with the Church.

A hidden journey of the spirit

This understanding of faith, and of the maps to faith, puts more emphasis on mystery than on biblical narratives or the usual language of doctrine. Because of this Rahner's writings have annoyed some traditional thinkers; but on the other hand they have appealed to many people who have been disappointed or turned off by too many religious words. He managed to speak to spiritual seekers in need of a slower journey to explicit faith through zones of silence and of desire, or through the options of their lives. This faith journey from within the spiritual adventure of one's life rings true for large numbers of people who feel themselves on the margins of the Church. In this sense Rahner is a subterranean theologian, one who directs attention to the Spirit working within us at levels deeper than creeds and concepts. He offers a different catechism, not of the content of faith in first place, but of the wavelength of its reception. Like many other theologians explored in these chapters, he moves the agenda of faith from outer to inner, but always rooting his vision in the basic reality of God's universal grace at work in humanity.

Against this background one can better understand Rahner's much quoted statement that future believers will have to be mystics or else they will not have faith (*TI*, VII, 15). Clearly this cannot mean that everyone will have the special gifts of mystical saints. Rather, it suggests that, in a more secular context, faith will need to be grounded in personal experience of grace. It will need an ability to discover the Spirit at work in one's ordinary life. In this sense everyone has the basis for being 'mystical', for 'an immediate encounter of the individual with God' (*KRD*, 176). We have only to become aware of this in-depth zone our lives and what it means: that God is already present in us long before we come to explicit faith; that we are *capax Dei*, or to use a more contemporary expression, 'wired for God'. As suggested in our diagram earlier, we are always invited by grace and oriented towards mystery.

Therefore a major element of any faith map lies within the hidden dimensions of daily human experience. As part of what Rahner called a 'brief creed' he wrote: 'the experience of God which is implicit in the experience of transcendence is not found in the first instance ... in theological reflection, but rather ... in our everyday acts of knowledge and freedom ... A person should be challenged to discover this universally present experience of God' (*FCF*, 454). And he adds that especially 'in the act of loving one's neighbour a person has an experience of God at least implicitly' (*FCF*, 456). Quite simply, God's grace is experienced within us. It is not something vaguely above us. So, if we pay attention to where we become more fully human, we are on the road to recognising both the God-given direction of our hearts and the daily drama of our interaction with God-as-grace.

The nearness of God

To awaken a sense of mystery seems an essential first stage in his map of faith. Like Newman, and like many more recent thinkers

about faith, Rahner opts for an inner journey of disposition as a
pastoral priority. But his ambitions lie elsewhere. He hopes to lead
people from what they live implicitly to an explicit and Christian
encounter with God. In fact he once said that all his theology was
meant to serve the 'kerygma' or proclamation of the Good News of
Christ.

Due to his particular emphasis on the *humanum*, Rahner has
sometimes been accused of getting stuck at the level of human
mystery, a charge that he strongly rebutted in interviews towards
the end of his life. He attacked the tendency to stress the 'relevance'
of faith for humanity and commented that a merely 'anthropocentric' approach represents a dangerous forgetfulness of God and
'absolute nonsense' as an interpretation of his theology (*ein abso-
luter Unsinn*). We needed to stop talking about God as existing for
us, in order to realise that we exist for God. And in response to
those who criticised his approach to faith he added: 'My aim is to
be a theologian who says that God is the most important reality
there is, that we exist to love him in a self-forgetting way, to adore
him, to exist for him, to soar beyond our existence into the abyss of
the ungraspable God ... To God we must entrust ourselves with
Jesus Crucified in unconditional surrender' (*KRD*, 267–268 translation slightly changed).

For Rahner the climax of God's self-giving happens when
Mystery comes to meet us in the person of Jesus Christ. 'This
radical mystery is nearness and not distance, self-surrendering love
and not a judgement' (*TI*, V, 7). But in spite of this intimate
nearness, God remains mystery, hidden, different, never captured
by our images or ideas. Rahner, more than some other theologians,
starts the faith journey with an invitation to attend to the 'mystery
of humanity' (to use an expression of *Gaudium et Spes*) in order to
glimpse the creative presence of grace in every life. If he emphasises
the faith journey 'from below', the reason for this is not simply its
relevance for modern culture, but because he sees humanity as
essentially graced and therefore deeply religious – in the sense that
God is permanently and universally present to us and leading us
towards life and love. Attention to the human spirit is a crucial
entry point, but with the further goal of discovering God as the
source of the orientation of our hearts. Late in life he described his

vision of faith as grounded in the real 'presence of the liberating Spirit' (*KRD*, 298).

In the voice of Rahner (an imaginary monologue)

When I want to help you to find God, I invite you to begin within yourself. Is that surprising? It is the road of many great saints, including Augustine. I am convinced that the road towards God passes through the desires of your heart, simply because those desires are placed there by God.

If you pause and enter into yourself, if you can create a space of quiet self-presence, you get in touch with your longing for something more, even for something infinite. You discover yourself as a kind of mystery, limited in one little life, yet open to infinite horizons of questions and questings. You are like a river in movement. Stillness in itself does not satisfy. Your self-presence on its own is not enough. If you come into yourself, paradoxically, you will discover a need to move out of yourself. Some 'beyond' beckons, as if the river of your life is flowing towards the sea, drawn powerfully towards the ocean that it has never yet seen. So if you really accept the mystery of your own self, it will guide you gradually to divine mystery.

I am not saying that this inner journey is easy. Far from it. Many of us can get caught in surface living or in the pressures of the practical. We want to escape the costly strangeness of this voyage within. What is deepest in us can easily get suppressed or avoided or neglected. If so, that zone of our self as a place of wonder remains unvisited, and this road to God remains untravelled.

Our main encounter with God

In fact, that desire to go beyond yourself is not your own doing. It is God's Spirit at work in the depths of each person. If you start with yourself, I am convinced that you can discover the hidden and creative treasure called grace. It is not a passive treasure but a vibrant source of your hope to live with love. Ultimately with God's own love.

Let me confess two difficulties of mine. Number one: I am often afraid of God-talk as practised by theologians and preachers. Not only because it can sound predictable and tired, almost like a dead language. More seriously, it can put the cart before the horse. It can lead people to think of God as a Big Object out there beyond us. But God is utterly close to us and yet silent, wanting to lead us to the Love that became humanly real for us in Christ. We could be looking in the wrong direction for the wrong god.

And here is my second difficulty: for the vast majority of humanity who have lived on this planet for thousands of years, a fullness of Christian faith was not possible. Even for the baptised and believing, I am convinced that our main contact with God is through a quiet grace that guides us through each ordinary day, rather than through explicit moments of religious awareness. What flowers into the fullness of Christian faith has its roots within us long before we come to hear the Word of revelation. Before the Word reaches its climax in the Gospel, the Spirit was already at work in all humanity, all cultures, all religions.

So too in each of us: the Spirit is always leading us towards an encounter with Christ, even though we are unaware of that guidance. We can notice the fruits even when we do not name the roots. That is why I encourage you to become aware of the direction of the river of your life. In spite of egoism and closure, you can recognise your yearning for goodness, and your living out of goodness in the concrete life of each day. In spite of shadows and refusals, you can become more open to love, passionate about truth, courageous in difficulties, generous in attitudes and actions, even surprisingly serene in the face of death itself. Can you recall a time when you were accused wrongly and managed not to react with bitterness, but even with understanding of the misunderstanding? Such signs are precious. They are evidence of the Spirit at work in your life. They show that the flow of your river is towards the ocean that is mystery, love, God. And this can be true of many people who cannot make sense of 'religion' as they perceive it. This hidden strand of our spiritual adventure is our normal experience of God. Not just our journey in the direction of God, but God's journey towards us, God's hidden revelation, like an artist secretly shaping our lives into love.

A movement into freedom

This road of grace is not always easy to discover. When you are really at peace, listening to the heart is not difficult. But there are also moments of weariness and emptiness, of scepticism and almost of despair, when it takes courage to enter the barren landscape of one's soul. The bitterness of existence can hit you in all sorts of ways. Don't be too surprised when such shadows come. They will not last. They are never the whole story. Dawn will come after every darkness. And that emergence into light is one of the signs of the Spirit at work. It is more than 'natural'. It is a healing liberation that comes from the artistry of God within us. In countless ways you experience God even though you may not realise it.

In these moments of renewed hope, when your inner self moves from pain into trust, that quiet transformation of your spirit comes from the creativity of the Spirit of God. If you learn to read the everyday in this light, you have an inner compass for your faith. When you learn to recognise the movements of the Spirit in your own responses, you are made ready for Christ. That fullness of revelation is more likely to come alive for today if people start from this slow expansion into love, where the Spirit is already preparing the epiphany of Christ.

Of course, our hyperactivity can keep us adrift on the surfaces of ourselves and unable to reach deeper levels of desire. So we need to prepare the way of the Lord, as the Gospel says, through attending to our own mystery first. It is never just our own mystery: it is the place where God pitches a tent in our deepest self. Here in this space our map to faith begins. Here our spirit can blossom into wonder before the mystery of ourselves. 'I thank you for the wonder of my being', says Psalm 138. Through such human openings we glimpse the greater mystery of God's self-giving to us in Christ. When we take time to pause and listen to our hearts, in the surprise of silence we find ourselves encountering more than the mystery of our small life. We experience our desire for something more than outer living. I would say that here, so to speak, we run into God and can become in a sense everyday mystics.

Let me put it another way. I said earlier that our usual encounters with God are not religious. You don't have to go into a church or pray or think about God in order to meet God. Those spaces are vital to nourish and deepen our faith, if we are believers. But whether we are believers or not, our experience of God is going on all the time in our choices and in our adventure of self-becoming. Here, even in small ways, our lives become works of art, works of love, through a co-operation with the Spirit of God who dwells within us. What can seem first (our own freedom) is in fact second: what is always first is the grace of God active in each human heart. This graced unfolding of our freedom is more fundamental than our reflections or our beliefs. It is where most people meet God.

To learn to read our lives in this spirit is what I mean by becoming a mystic for today. If someone were to follow this road I can imagine him or her voicing their experience something like this:

> In the adventure of my humanity, I have sensed the guidance of God's mystery, close to me and creative in me. I have come to discover God as an artist's presence in the adventure of my life. In the flow of my daily choices, I have recognised the healing touch of Christ, eroding my ego into generosity in hidden ways. In the silence of my heart I know something of the artistry of the Spirit, shaping my life towards a love beyond my imagining. And all this experience of grace, in the theatre of the ordinary, is a pull towards newness that my words can never express.

Christ as dazzling light

Some people tell me that I over-stress the human and that we should begin with Christ. Of course we should, *if* it is culturally possible and pastorally fruitful. In other words if it meets the sensibility and needs of people. But, just as St Paul was called to preach to the Gentiles, I am thinking of so many today who can be 'turned off' by this direct approach. My passion has always been to make Christ real for those on the margins of faith or church. And that is why I prefer the 'anthropological' approach (not to be confused with anthropo*centric*).

Five years before my death the new Pope, John Paul II, published his first encyclical, a passionate and personal text about humanity, entitled *Redemptor hominis*, or *Redeemer of Humanity*. It is, in part, a hymn of praise to Christ who, like a mirror of wonder, discloses to us who we really are. With great force the Pope insisted that attention to the full drama of humanity was 'the way for the Church', because 'Christ is in a way united, even when people are unaware of it', with every human being 'without any exception whatever'. The Pope repeated that last expression twice in once sentence (§ 14). I find myself totally in tune with this generous vision of our mystery, but there is another sentence that gives me even greater consolation. At one point John Paul II invites everyone to discover Christ not only in prayer but through 'deep wonder' at one's own self, and he adds: 'the name for that deep amazement at human worth and dignity is the Gospel' (§ 10). It is the order of the Pope's sentence that strikes me most. What starts as human wonder comes to be recognised as Good News: Christ brings into dazzling light the gift that was already present in the depths of every life. As St Ignatius said at the end of his famous prayer, that is enough for me.

References to works of Karl Rahner

FCF   *Foundations of Christian Faith*, New York, 1978.

KRD *Karl Rahner in Dialogue: conversations and interviews 1965–1982*, New York, 1986.

TI   *Theological Investigations*, 23 Volumes, London and New York, 1961–1992.

4

Hans Urs von Balthasar: the drama of beauty

By any reckoning, Balthasar must be counted among the greats of modern theology and his perspective differs from many of the other thinkers examined in this book. Where most of them focus on our spiritual quest for meaning and ultimately for God, Balthasar views this as ignoring what is essential to Christian faith. Why begin from humanity if God has spoken? Why start from our desires if God has desired us and loved us in Christ? In a secularised culture it may be understandable to start 'from below', because dormant spiritual senses need awakening. But to concentrate on human searching could miss the uniqueness of revelation, which is less about human need than about divine action. So Balthasar gives priority to the majestic love embodied in Jesus. To recognise this entails a world-shattering glimpse of 'glory', beside which all 'anthropological' approaches fade into second place. An encounter with the love disclosed in Christ changes the whole agenda of faith and takes us beyond any typical talk about credibility: 'true love is always incomprehensible, and only so is it gratuitous' (*LA*, 44).

Balthasar started his academic life in the field of literature, devoting years to a thesis on the apocalypse of the German soul. His goal was to discern a hidden presence of Christ in literary works, and at this early stage of his thinking he gave much emphasis to individual consciousness. However, he abandoned this approach after a spiritual conversion that remained with him for the rest of his life. During a spiritual retreat he came to realise the utter 'objectivity' of Christ and from then on he became wary of all subjective approaches to religion. Having detected in his own sensibility an attraction for this human starting point, he later became convinced of its limitations. Thus faith, in his view, meant above all 'making space for the gift of God' (*GL*, VII, 308).

In a text written in old age Balthasar sums up his life-long preference: 'we do not begin by reflecting on ourselves but by responding to the fact that we have been addressed and called by this divine miracle' (*TL*, III, 364) Here we have the basis of his long tussle with Karl Rahner. Their priorities were radically different, largely because their interpretation of the religious needs of today were different. Rahner feared jumping into explicit faith language without preparing the ground well, without evoking the mystery of our humanity as a place of God's presence. Balthasar was afraid that too much focus on this human road could postpone or evade the overwhelming surprise of Christ.

Late in his life, Balthasar remarked that his disagreements with Rahner stemmed from two conflicting godfathers of German thought – Kant and Goethe. Kant, to simplify drastically, studied the operations of the thinking subject as shaping our sense of reality, and so he elevated the self as a source of value and truth. Goethe, on the other hand, celebrated life's mystery as unity. Against the excessive clarities of rationalism he defended the role of religious sensibility (even though he was not an orthodox believer, as Kant was). Balthasar saw Kant as a source of the subjectivism he detected in Rahner, resulting in too central a role for self-transcendence and its fulfilment. But he praised Goethe for protecting our capacity for wonder and beauty, essential qualities, in Balthasar's view, towards glimpsing the glory of God in Christ. Ultimately a Christian 'is in love with the love that appeared in Christ' (*LA*, 107).

The perception of glory

The early volumes of Balthasar's work deal with the perception of God's beauty; a second phase goes on to explore the drama of our freedom in answering God's call. These two moments – of recognition and response – are central to the experience of faith as he understands it. Moving away from the intellectualism of the scholastic tradition, he looks to aesthetics, or the encounter with overwhelming beauty, as the model for recognising God's love in Christ. Then distancing himself from the cold moralism of previous theology, he looks to the tradition of theatre to present faith as the interaction of two freedoms (God's and ours). Christianity, he insists, is not primarily 'a communication of knowledge' but a revelation of 'God's action', continuing the biblical drama between God and humanity (*LA*, 58).

Like other theologians explored in these chapters, Balthasar reacts strongly against approaching faith rationalistically and from the outside. Echoing Newman, he stresses its intensely personal and self-involving nature, always needing an attitude of receptivity and reverence. He wants us to see faith more as God's doing rather than ours, because 'faith perceives God's light' and participates in the 'self-disclosure of God's interior life and light' (*GL*, I, 150, 157). Hence we should abandon any merely external faith map. Balthasar attacks older forms of apologetics as drastically flawed, because they made philosophical reasons for God preparatory for a possible act of faith. He described this school as 'joyless', as 'torn between knowing and believing', especially because it had no appreciation of 'the dimension of aesthetic contemplation' (*GL*, I, 174).

In older philosophy, beauty was one of the universal concepts or 'transcendentals', together with truth, goodness and unity; but under the influence of modernity truth became isolated from these companions, and especially from beauty. Balthasar's focus on beauty seeks to retrieve neglected dimensions in the experience of faith, insisting that God's revelation invites us to a kind of ecstasy, akin to the experience of great art. But this beauty is not of this world: in Balthasar's words, the 'beauty of God' is glimpsed only when love is perceived as 'the core of everything' (*GL*, VII, 19) and when this recognition expands into rapture. We are taken out of ourselves by what we glimpse in Christ, where 'inner light and outer form' (*GL*, VII, 315) converge to create a unique radiance, what traditionally has been called 'glory'.

Although that much-used word can ring rather hollow or vaguely religious, in the Biblical tradition glory is a key concept, evoking moments of epiphany or fullness when the greatness of God is felt – as mystery, as different, as transforming, and as beyond all our usual language. Even more extraordinary is the climax of Christ's story, where glory, beauty and the Cross come together. Here a different glory enters history. Seeking to refresh our sense of beauty and glory, Balthasar draws on St Paul concerning the 'glory of God in the face of Christ' (2 Cor. 4:6), which becomes a key text for him. This love is at its most glorious in the darkness of the Passion, and the momentum of this glory continues at the heart of Christian faith. 'As an attitude, faith is the surrender of one's own experience to the experience of Christ', including his 'non-experience' of death (*GL*, I, 412).

In their more secular sense beauty and glory are often associated with magnificence, power and even pomp. But in Christ Crucified everything changes tone. If there is majesty, it is powerless and vulnerable. 'The boundless love of God' is both 'poor' and 'power-less' (*GL*, VII, 352). If there is power, it has nothing to do with our ordinary logic of control or dominance. What is specifically Christian begins where our usual ideas fall silent, when we are faced with the humanly unimaginable, and when God's love speaks to our hearts through the dying and rising of Christ.

A different logic

Linked with this 'theological aesthetic' of faith is a 'theocentric' rather than an 'anthropocentric theory of knowledge' (*TL*, I, 262). As already seen, Balthasar rejected the notion that we arrive at faith through two successive stages of inquiry, first rational and then religious. Instead he proposes a core logic of 'believing trust' (*TL*, I, 261) and of openness to mystery, an approach grounded in the priority of love over knowledge. Without this priority we fall into the external reasoning of the serpent in the Book of Genesis, who 'presents truth as thinglike' (*TL*, I, 262). Balthasar hoped to help an atheistic culture to 'learn to *see* again, which is to say, to experience the total otherness of Christ as the outshining of God's sublimity and glory' (TL, I, 20). At Balthasar's funeral in 1988, the then Cardinal Ratzinger preached, quoting a sermon of St Augustine as encapsulating the focus of the great Swiss theologian: 'Our entire task in this life consists in healing the eyes of the heart that they may be able to see God'.

Such an emphasis broadens 'the problem of credibility' inherited from past centuries with its 'narrowly conceived and controversial notion of faith' (*LA*, 16). Balthasar's approach calls us, in the spirit of Newman and others, to liberate our model of knowing from empiricist philosophies of truth, and from any philosophy that divorces truth from love. Knowing, in existential or religious questions, has an ethical dimension and cannot be separated from love both as gift and as the source of truth. In Balthasar's words, 'the very existence of truth, of eternal truth, is grounded in love' (*TL*, I, 272) and there can be 'no cold objectivity in love' (*TL*, I, 266). Thus he sees faith as a participation in God's own self-knowing and Trinitarian love. Is this 'high' vision so unworldly that it risks seeming distant from the language of ordinary searchers? It is not unfair to say that whereas Rahner's more humanist approach seems able to reach unbelievers, Balthasar's richly spiritual account of faith makes sense more easily to those who are already believers.

The drama of freedom

As already mentioned, a first stage of Balthasar's exploration of faith seeks to present our encounter with revelation as an experience of beauty, where we perceive the presence of God in Christ. A second stage moves on to the drama of freedom at the heart of faith. It would be inadequate to think of faith simply as a perception of God's love in Christ. That perception leads into to a whole adventure of lived faith, starting from that amazement before beauty but going further: God's revelation is not just an object to contemplate but a call into the mission and action of God in history.

   Therefore in Balthasar's great trilogy, the first series of volumes deals with faith as the perception of beauty, but the second series takes the analogy of theatre in order to reflect on the dramatic dimension of Christian existence. The wonder born from the initial encounter with beauty now gives way to the struggle of discipleship. If at first my wavelength is transformed by the glory of love, this leads to a more purifying stage – the transformation of my freedom. God is more ambitious for me than I might want. Faith is never just a source of aesthetic joy: it becomes a battleground between my unconverted heart and the hopes of Christ for me. Faith goes beyond consoling peace and becomes movement. We are 'drawn into the action', as in a theatre, where 'we have been appointed to play our part' in a huge drama, which is nothing less than God's 'action in and upon the world' (*TD*, I, 15–17). To share in Christ's work and mission will entail a long and costly conversion of the ego, and so faith becomes a life-long drama of personal and indeed social praxis.

Balthasar sees God as 'the main character' in a great drama, which is also a story of 'our appropriation' of faith (*TD*, II, 17). The emphasis moves from perception to a call to action. If an initial moment of faith echoes those interpersonal or aesthetic moments when we are invited into sheer wonder, now the adventure goes further: 'no one is enraptured without returning, from this encounter, with a personal mission' (*TD*, II, 31). God enters the scene as the artist not only of personal lives but of all struggling human history. This is what genuine spirituality has always known and acknowledged: 'the drama of a life lived in discipleship of Christ has remained alive down the centuries'. But 'the manuals of dogmatics' paid little attention to this drama of faith as lived (*TD*, II, 168). As against this damaging forgetfulness, Balthasar wants to recognise and respond to 'Christ's continuing action', so that faith is seen again as 'the progressive growth of one's own existence into Christ's existence' (*GL*, I, 224).

A note of conflict

It is a simplification but not untrue to distinguish two schools in modern theology, sometimes labelled 'dialectical' or 'correlational'. The correlational tendency stresses continuity between nature and grace, or between human and divine, as exemplified in different ways in Rahner or Tillich. Balthasar belonged more to the opposite or dialectical school, stressing ways in which faith is both different and demanding. Just as there was conflict in the Gospel, in the life and death of Jesus, faith will always involve a struggle in each person who wants to follow Him. To be a Christian means to walk a different road, one that could even lead to martyrdom.

In this light what we call 'glory' becomes more disconcerting. It invites us beyond our comfort zones into a realm of divine immensity that can never fit into our ways of imagining God. The rapture that Balthasar speaks of is also rupture. The revelation of love in Christ takes the road to Jerusalem and death, and its victory in Resurrection can be enjoyed only as a transforming light emerging from an appalling darkness. 'A terrible beauty is born' is a famous line in a poem by Yeats. It could be adapted to fit Balthasar: what seems terrible, the public execution of a criminal, conceals the most extraordinary beauty the world has known, where God's self-giving explodes into the glory of a love alive forever. What seems (and is) tragic becomes the supreme revelation of God's love. 'It is precisely in the Kenosis of Christ (and nowhere else) that the *inner* majesty of God's love appears' (*LA*, 71).

Faith, to repeat, is principally receptivity and recognition on our part of what God has done and continues to do in Christ. Desire and decision remain essential in the human adventure of faith but they are not the foundation stones. The historical initiative of God is the key to Christian faith. Faith 'entrusts itself to the reality and the possibility of absolute love' (*GL*, VII, 377) and this becomes the source of 'all love between human persons' (*GL*, VII, 376). In this way the momentum of love is complete: what starts within God as Trinity, and what we glimpse in Christ, becomes through us as Church a new love to transform our wounded world.

Faith as a Yes to a Yes

This remains a powerful but austere vision. Perhaps it can only be grasped within a certain contemplative wonder and silence, where revelation invites us to a recognition that 'all is grace' (as Thérèse of Lisieux and Bernanos both insisted). All the multifaceted aspects of the mystery – the love of the Trinity, the shock of the Cross, the glory of Resurrection, the outpouring of the Spirit into our struggling history – all this richness calls for a simplicity of heart that receives and adores and is gradually transformed. Faith in this vision is indeed a Yes to a Yes. The first Yes is God's, steady, eternal, and then embodied in Christ. The second Yes is ours, unsteady, unfocused, yet learning to live with a strength that is not ours. 'Faith is never a possession held in tranquility, but a struggle, a decision, a stranding up to be counted ... its core is the unfathomable love of God for us, which continually fills us with such new bliss and terror that we must let everything go in order to take hold of it alone' (*ET*, III, 83).

Akin to the other religious writers explored in these chapters, Balthasar shares the goal of rethinking the foundations of faith. 'To give reasons for one's hope', for all of these authors, means liberating and deepening the agenda. They all resist the dominance of impersonal reasoning (which seemed the only acceptable avenue to truth in 'modernity') and they seek to broaden the horizon to include the whole person. But, as already seen, Balthasar shifts the focus from the capacities and dispositions of the seeker of faith to the unique content of revelation, and in particular to the disclosure of the truth, goodness and beauty of God in Christ. No matter what road we travel towards faith, it is crucial to remember the mountain peak we hope to reach. The God we are talking about remains, painfully and yet beautifully, beyond all our best words and our deepest imagining.

Application to today's culture: a personal reflection

Before attempting to 'translate' Balthasar for today, imagining his own possible words, a short personal reflection may help. Here I want to acknowledge the healthy challenge that Balthasar offers to our post-Vatican II generation. Modern thinking has been dominated by the 'turn to the subject'. Insofar as Balthasar tried to purify the excesses of this school and to initiate a 'return to the object', his work questions deeply-rooted assumptions in the culture around us and even in our personal living of faith. Under the influence of my literary training (a parallel with Balthasar) and then of the cultural revolution that religious life experienced in the 1960s and 1970s, my spirituality certainly became more subjective. Quietly, a whole tradition of asceticism was set aside, not only in the sense of abandoning external austerities, but of allowing self-fulfillment to replace self-sacrifice as a core value. Our generation discovered self-expression and affectivity. All this was exciting and worthwhile, and yet, on reflection, in danger of being one-sided. Almost imperceptibly we came to live a new set of priorities, where the subjective aspect of religion became stronger than the objective. Even prayer was often judged in terms of experience (initially a positive revaluing of a neglected dimension). 'How do I feel' became a litmus paper for growth.

If I recognise how this new sensibility influenced spirituality, the reading of Balthasar raises awkward but important questions. His emphasis on 'objectivity' invites me to make room again for adoration and for obedient reverence for God. This breaks the magnifying glass of subjectivism. His language of faith reminds me that the glory of God is greater than any possible response of mine. The glory that shines in the face of Christ is indeed a call to 'humanity fully alive' (to echo Irenaeus) but that glory goes beyond self-measured fullness, because it is the radiance of the Crucified Jesus as Risen Lord. It stands over against me rather as a great work of art, that moves me, but is always itself, not dependent on me for its power or beauty. In Balthasar's words (in one of his numerous evocations of the experience of art as a parallel for the experience of faith): 'the originality of a work of art' can only be perceived 'by the impression it gives of complete inevitability with perfect freedom, overwhelming the beholder, and making one say: it could only have been thus' (*ET*, I, 180)

In the voice of Balthasar (an imaginary monologue)

> After a mother has smiled for some time
> at her child, it will begin to smile back;
> she has awakened love in its heart (*LA*, 61).

At various moments of my life I developed a simple human example to illustrate the nature of Christian faith. I asked my readers to ponder an infant's first smile. Parents especially will vividly recall this magical and yet ordinary moment, which usually does not arrive until the second month of a baby's life. Why did this event happening seem so important to me? Because it is a perfect symbol of the structure of faith. That first smile is a response to a gift already received. The love that welcomed the infant into life is now recognised and the smile is the expression of that recognition. Of course the word infant comes from the Latin word for speechless (*infans*), and it will be a long time before the new baby will speak real words. But this smile is a primal language of wonder, of gratitude, and, I would argue, of freedom. This is the first moment not only of recognition of love but of a human response to love. The gift of love is received from beyond the self, from the care of mother and father and others around, and this now gives birth to a response of grateful trust. For the first time the infant comes to awareness, to relationship, awakening to that gift and joyfully expressing a 'yes'. And that is exactly what faith is like.

In this light I always wanted to stress that love comes before faith, and indeed that faith means acknowledging a love already surrounding us. Other important dimensions such as beliefs, creeds, church belonging and so on, enter later, just as language enters the life of the child later. But the core of faith is like that smile, an awakening to a gift ready received and that continues to be received.

Another important strand in my vision of faith stems from my formation and perhaps from my temperament. From my early years and then as a young student I was immersed in the worlds of literature and music. This aesthetic horizon shaped me before I came to study theology. Through my experience of masterpieces of human creativity, I realised how the over-whelming power of beauty can lead us into new spaces of awe and openness. At first I was attracted by the subjective experi-ence of art, relishing its impact on me, but then I came to realise that my aesthetic experience was secondary. What was primary was the sheer splendour of the work itself. There is a glory present in the flow of a Mozart symphony or in the power of Goethe's writings. It remains itself, magnificently independ-ent of me. Indeed its existence challenges and judges me, like that Rilke poem where he gazes at a broken statue of Apollo in Paris, and the statue seems to say to him: you must change your life. Beauty transforms us, if we allow it.

When I came to study undergraduate theology for the first time, it was horrifying. At that time everything was decadently scholastic – definitions, dogmas, heresies, and all in Latin. Where was the glory of God? Nowhere to be found in that approach. And yet intuitively I knew that God's revelation was more like music than like the dry conclusions I was offered by my professors. I remember stuffing my ears with cotton wool during lectures and reading Saint Augustine! Here I discov-ered passion and beauty and a sense of the drama of faith. In him and in other thinkers on faith from the early centuries I discovered another way of speaking of faith. I began to have confidence that we could emerge from the prison house of scholasticism through exploring God as beautiful.

If my need to distance myself from the dull theology of the textbooks was clear from the beginning, another discernment took more time. Others of my generation were developing new languages for faith and for theology. They were moving towards more personal and spiritual approaches. Some of them were much influenced by the tradition that came down from Kant and that stressed the subjective operations of the mind searching for meaning. This was helpful for many people, because it seemed rang true to their inner journey, by focusing on the dynamism of desire. However, I began to have doubts about it. It reminded me of my own youthful tendency to stress the effect of art on me rather than the beauty of art in itself. I came to find this whole approach too subjective. Why spend time in the foothills of human searching, when you can open the door to God who knocks and wants to disclose another vision of everything?

Therefore in all of my work I tried to give attention to the objective glory of Christ. 'Objective' is a difficult and even dangerous word, especially if it suggests something that stands out there, away from me. I wanted to change the emphasis from ourselves to what we receive and perceive as God's revelation. In that sense, I sought to change the focus from 'subjective' exploring to 'objective' contemplation of God's love. And so we come back to that first smile and to how the gift, by its very nature, comes before any acceptance and response. The starting point for faith lies not in us but in the gift of God. I do not want to disparage faith maps that focus on our desire. But I sensed that the faith crisis of today's culture could best be met by delving deeper. The typical horizons of our own thinking will not bring us to faith, because it is a gift from beyond us. And so I devoted my energies to what was unique in Christ, and to how we might perceive or receive that revelation.

The cost of freedom

If I was hesitant about excessively subjective approaches to faith, I was equally so about interpretations that appeared to soften the shock of the Gospel. Faith is more than recognition of beauty: it involves response, transformation, drama. I learned from my great mentor, Karl Barth, to stress the unity of two sides of faith: the aspect of joy and the aspect of the Cross. On the one hand, I tried to bring out the beauty of revelation and faith (as against older and colder ways of theology); on the other, that beauty finds its unexpected fullness in the Cross of Christ. It is into this darkness that love descended. So a joyful perception of love (the first smile) is not the whole story of faith. Sooner or later we meet shadows and even tragedy, and so we find ourselves in the theatre of our freedom. What God reveals in Christ goes beyond all our imagining in its beauty, but its differentness disturbs all our normal horizons.

Inevitably we resist this full range of love, and yet God's freedom is at work in us to set free our struggling freedom. Faith at times will ask a surrender of our experience into the hands of Christ. A first stage of faith can be suffused with light: it can enjoy a blessed encounter with love which provokes that smile of grateful acceptance. But other moments of faith will entail a more agonised acceptance, trusting that as we lose our lives, in many different ways, if we are with Christ, losing can mean finding. Yes, faith entails a recognition of love, but a love that is more costly than cosy, for us as it was for Christ.

Of course the cost of the Cross was not the final act in the drama of the Gospels, nor is it for us. At the centre of our faith shines the radiance of the Crucified Jesus as Risen Lord. Before Him all our questing and questioning are like minor themes in a great symphony, important in their own wandering way, but relativised when the Gospel offers us a richer map of faith and when words such as 'beauty' and 'glory' take on new life, one that opens into eternity.

Prayer as learning space

Perhaps I can make all this more concrete through our experience of prayer. Indeed if theology does not sometimes speak of
prayer, or nourish our paths of prayer, there must be something
wrong with it. I often mentioned the need for a 'praying
theology' because our deepest knowledge does not come from
thinking but from our receiving of love, and because prayer is
the place where that receiving happens most fruitfully. If
someone is trying to move from unbelief to faith, my invitation
to him or her is not only to read or ponder about it, but rather to
risk the exposure that is prayer. 'Come and see', as Jesus used
to say.

Prayer, in this spirit, is not an exercise in thinking or speaking but in listening and openness. Ultimately your can only
know God through God, as an always ungraspable Love.
Prayer is where you allow God to act and to become real,
beyond your small agendas of understanding. You gradually
realise that your inner life is not the measure of God. We are
not the starting point for prayer: God is. And the same is true
for faith. You learn that fulfillment comes from receiving rather
than from constructing or striving.

I repeat: a vital transformation takes place when you stop
focusing on your own experience and relax into the quietly
overwhelming gift of God's presence. Prayer is no longer your
effort but becomes God's initiative. An inner Copernican
revolution takes place: you are freed from the burden of being
the centre of your universe, as you become a simple receiver
of Christ's 'fullness', 'grace upon grace' (John 1:16). Whenever
subjective experience ceases to be the criterion of reality, the
inherited wound of modernity is healed. In both prayer and
faith the typical 'modern' spirit of mastery is humbled. The
flow of the river of desire is reversed, because now God
desires to take over, in a silence that is both gentle and
powerful. Here God does what God does best, which is
resurrection, so that we can rise into loving with God.

I began with the image of the first smile as a symbol of faith.
What the first smile and prayer have in common is very

simple: first we receive Love and then we can respond with love. And here we glimpse a glory and a beauty that not only calls us, but empowers us to a different way of life, to a daily discipleship. Faith makes sense from inside that movement of love.

References to works of Hans Urs von Balthasar

ET   *Explorations in Theology*, 3 volumes, San Francisco, 2000–2005

GL   *The Glory of the Lord*, 7 volumes, Edinburgh, 1982–1991.

LA   *Love Alone: the Way of Revelation*, London, 1968.

TD   *Theo-Drama*, 5 volumes, San Francisco, 1988–1998.

TL   *Theo-Logic*, 3 volumes, San Francisco, 2000–2005.

5

Bernard Lonergan: guidance towards gift

If Bernard Lonergan remains one of the largely unknown giants of twentieth-century theology, the reason is not hard to find. He dedicated himself so much to the foundations of theology and philosophy that his work never reached a wide public. Even today there are many professional theologians who have little acquaintance with his writings. Yet others regard this Canadian Jesuit as a genius who in time will come to be recognised as such. Here the aim is to pick out certain aspects of his work seeking, as in other chapters, to discern what light he offers for our faith journeys today.

Lonergan described himself as a conservative thinker, impatient with anyone who would throw out the baby with the bathwater. He himself came to realise gradually, and painfully, that the sands were shifting for religious faith, and that theology as it had been taught was hopelessly out of touch. It had lived outside history in a realm of unchanging and permanent truths, whereas a whole new world had come to birth. We needed to face 'a crisis not of faith but of culture' (*C*, 244). At the intellectual level the old criteria of truth required rethinking. At a social level a new life style left people without religious roots of belonging. So he set himself to respond to this crisis of culture by exploring the basics of knowing in general and of faith in particular.

New foundations

In about 1965, after years of study and teaching, he proposed a new foundation for theology that was a major surprise for some people; and yet, on reflection, it seems so obvious. Instead of starting to ponder faith or do theology from scriptural revelation or from statements of Church authority, he concluded that especially for today's empirical culture, theology needs grounding in the religious experience of being transformed by God's love.

But let us go back in time, to understand something of his theory of how we arrive at truth. In 1929, when Lonergan was a twenty-four-year-old student of philosophy in England, he came across Newman's *Grammar of Assent* and read it six times. Already this young Canadian was aware of problems arising from modern science and of how old-style Catholic thinking failed to meet these challenges. Of all the major theologians of the twentieth century, he was the only one with a specialist understanding of science. So his youthful questions came from a different perspective. How can we justify judgements of truth in areas that are not just empirical, such as faith? How can we get beyond the typical modern image of the 'real' – as something 'out there now' that can be confirmed by taking a good look? If this 'picture thinking' is the only acceptable method, faith is in deep trouble.

Lonergan's early encounter with Newman set him on a journey of exploration that would last the rest of his life. In particular he found himself attracted by the psychological introspection of the great Cardinal. As seen in our first chapter, to defend Christian faith a neutral approach of 'proofs' was self-defeating. The questioner has to pay attention to the inner operations involved in arriving at truth, and has to be personally involved in the search. Thus Lonergan, initially under the influence of Newman and later of Aquinas, developed an approach that coincides in some ways with Karl Rahner. Both of them brought religious experience back into theology and both are often labelled as belonging to the school of 'transcendental Thomism'. But Lonergan's analysis of the process of faith is more precise and definite, more Anglo-Saxon one might say.

The Ladder of Knowing

His first rule was simply 'pay attention', in the sense of becoming aware of the dynamism of how you know and how you decide. You experience something. You ask questions about it. You reflect on your hunch. You go on to a judgement about its truth. You move to another level of 'so what'? What are you to do about it? How can you choose the right path? With such deceptively simple questions Lonergan went back to philosophy to rebuild the foundations of religious truth and to prepare the way for his later work on method in theology. The result was the enormous book called *Insight: a study of human understanding*.

There are dangers in offering such a short summary of his basic concerns. To some it could all sound simple and obvious. To others it may seem just a theory. Lonergan always challenged his students and his readers to engage in what he called 'self-appropriation'. Simply to read through *Insight* would be futile if the reader does not continually verify the 'cognitional structure' in his own experience and reflection. The main object is 'to discover oneself in oneself' (*M*, 260) and so to change one's understanding of understanding. More ambitious still, Lonergan's goal was to liberate us from certain dominant assumptions of our culture that equate knowing with external verification. If that is our main way of knowing, then God is off the map. There are no external data on God. But full human knowing takes us beyond the world of the senses.

According to Lonergan, science itself works from data through hypothesis to verification. However, verification is not achieved using the eyes, but through the human capacity to judge (what Newman had called the 'illative sense'). All human knowing travels that path: from experience through insight to judgement, and then beyond a judgement of truth to the possibility of moral or existential decisions. This map of human knowing became fundamental for Lonergan. It was his principal contribution to epistemology or philosophy of knowing. If St Ignatius offered 'spiritual exercises' in order to help people put focus into their lives and find God in prayer, in *Insight* Lonergan offered 'intellectual exercises' to help people identify essential steps in their process of knowing, and hence to become more secure about their ability to arrive at truth, including of course the truth of faith.

Impediments to freedom

But faith is not an ordinary truth. To recognise God is not the same as verifying an experiment. It invites us to levels of ourselves beyond the narrowly rational. The question of God, Lonergan came to see, can best be faced on the level of our freedom. But are we really free? He wrote eloquently about various blockages or forms of 'bias' that can leave us seriously unfree. 'There can be a love of darkness', resulting in a 'mist of obscurity ... of doubt and rationalization, of insecurity and disquiet' (*I*, 214–215). The assumptions of common sense can imprison us in small spaces. Questions can be lazily avoided or made to seem impossible. When a whole culture imposes blinkers on people, their deeper desires are smothered by a plethora of surface distractions. In this way the parable of the sower is re-enacted within the complexity of today's life-styles.

Lonergan explores three kinds of distortion that can obstruct the road to faith. The first, which he called 'individual bias', is the perennial tendency to put one's own self at the centre of the universe and to think and act accordingly. 'With startling modesty', he says with a touch of irony, 'one does not venture to raise the relevant further questions'; and even if the egoist is vaguely aware of self-deception, he usually manages to stifle any disquiet of conscience (*I*, 245). Such stunting of the drive of one's questions leaves a person unready for faith. Self-transcendence becomes blocked when one lives with 'egotistical disregard of others' (*M*, 53).

A second category called 'group bias' shows itself in prejudices connected with belonging to a section of society or of the planet. My outlook on life can be distorted by the perspective of my circle or sub-culture or part of the world. 'We' are always right and outsiders are viewed with suspicion. As René Girard might say, we feed on hostility and thus construct a negative identity for ourselves. In Lonergan's words, 'hostile groups do not easily forget their grievances, drop their resentment, overcome their fears' (*M*, 53). Hence group bias results in 'a blind spot for the insights that reveal its well-being to be excessive' (*I*, 248). Such a closed set of attitudes can paralyse the capacity for social change, including the source of transformation that is religious faith.

The third bias consists in a preference for short-term pragmatism, at the expense of ever getting to the roots of things. It is all too easy to live within a daily routine of practical concerns and to ignore any larger horizons. In Lonergan's words, 'common sense commonly feels itself omnicompetent ... and commonly is una-

ware of the admixture of common nonsense in its more cherished
convictions and slogans' (*M*, 53). Such short-sightedness, which
masquerades as common sense, can repress any question of God. If
the 'real' is what can be managed in the short-term, then God
comes to seem 'unreal'. The 'eros' or upward movement of desire in
every human being can be 'mutilated' unless it finds ways of
'stretching forth'. So all three forms of bias can stifle the 'native
orientation to the divine' (*M*, 103).

Lonergan, who was always fascinated by social and economic
history, offers a sombre reading of the modern world as urgently in
need of faith and redemption. In his view the outcome of bias is a
cumulative but unconscious compromise, both on the individual
and the cultural levels. If unrecognised, it produces impotence and
ideology and can even 'menace civilization with destruction' (*M*,
40). Where a communal flight from understanding happens, stag-
nation takes over and situations head towards crisis and perhaps
the tragedy of war. The freedom to imagine life differently disappears, and with it the spiritual freedom to believe that God could
have entered into the chaos of human history.

Being-in-love as transformation

By contrast with these distortions, Lonergan thought of faith in
terms of a healing conversion of horizons. Just as there is a need to
liberate ourselves from a reductive version of truth (the myth of the
out-there-now as the criterion of reality), so too there is a need to
revisit the roads towards human authenticity, of which religious
faith is the transforming crown – as we will see. If bias, in its triple
form, can produce a dangerous inauthenticity, what would authenticity look like?

It would be a flowering of self-transcendence through fidelity to
'the eros of the human spirit' (*M*, 13). This involves 'becoming a
person' (*M*, 104) by facing and answering our many levels of
questioning. And that process is not merely an intellectual exercise
because it takes us into the realm of freedom, including a fundamental choice about the goal of our lives. Lonergan often speaks of
the contrast between a life of drifting and a life of commitment to
values. The drifter is content to follow the crowd, without really

seizing the rudder of existence: 'content to think and say what everyone else is thinking and saying' (*C*, 224). But a person arrives at authentic freedom through an existential moment, through realising that it is up to oneself to decide what one is make of oneself. Responsibility for the quality of one's life is frighteningly in one's own hands. Existence becomes 'open-eyed', even though 'what has been achieved in always precarious: it can slip, fall, shatter'; nevertheless a person can emerge not only from drifting into self-ownership, but from the childhood world of immediacy to a 'world mediated by meaning' (*C*, 224–225). Here our horizons are expanded through shared traditions of value, of memory, of culture, of church. In fact Lonergan (like Charles Taylor) insists that 'the person is not the primordial fact. What is primordial is the community' (*PGT*, 211). Therefore it is within a tradition or culture that both of these transitions happen – from passivity to mature conscience, and from the immediacy of animal-like knowing to the larger world of meaning. And in this way we become ready for the gift of God's revelation, which is in fact 'God's own entry into man's world mediated by meaning' (*2C*, 260).

So far our journey towards authenticity has been described in terms of a human achievement of self-transcendence. The climax of this adventure has not yet been mentioned: it involves the peak of our freedom where another reality enters the scene. That reality is love. Lonergan speaks of the event of falling in love as opening a person to a new state of 'being-in-love', and of how this new horizon 'takes over' as the source of one's whole life (*M*, 105). The experience of love anchors a person's energies; it is the contrary of a life of drifting. 'When we fall in love life begins anew. A new principle takes over and, as long as it lasts, we are lifted above ourselves' (*3C*, 175). Of course love can take different forms. There is a love of intimacy between people, and there is also a 'being in love with God' which 'can be as full and as dominant, as overwhelming and as lasting an experience as human love' (*C*, 231).

It is significant that Lonergan explores the transformative power of love before coming to reflect on the nature of faith. More particularly he gives special attention to the 'religious experience' of being in love with God. For him this is the highest fulfilment of our capacity for self-transcendence: 'it takes over the peak of the soul'

(*M*, 107). Up to this point, our growth as persons is the fruit of fidelity to our questions and to our conscience. But now the agenda shifts from our *achievement* of authenticity to the surprise of a *gift* that changes everything. This new condition of being-in-love with God is never the product of our intelligence or freedom: 'on the contrary, it dismantles and abolishes the horizon in which our knowing and choosing went on and it sets up a new horizon in which the love of God will transvalue our values and the eyes of that love will transform our knowing' (*M*, 106). Ultimately this transforming love is something we receive, not something we bring about.

Faith as love-knowledge

In this way Lonergan seeks to translate the traditional theology of grace into the language of religious experience. As mentioned earlier, a major turning point in his thinking came around 1965 with his insight that a new foundation for theology lay in the 'radical transformation' that is 'fundamental to religious living' (*2C*, 65). Older theologies remained abstract and static, and paid little attention to this core of all religion. A theology worthy of today should give pride of place to the 'ongoing process' of 'living religion', because 'religion is conversion in its preparation, in its occurrence, in its developments, in its consequents, and also, alas, in its incompleteness, its failures, its breakdowns, its disintegration' (*2C*, 66–7). The authenticity (or inauthenticity) of religion depends on remaining in relationship (or not) with this disturbing and liberating gift of God's love.

How does this gift happen? Again and again Lonergan refers to his favourite verse from St Paul: 'the love of God is poured into our hearts by the Spirit given to us' (Rom. 5:5). This outpouring of the Spirit is universal, flowing secretly, so to speak, into every human heart. But God's love for us can remain unrequited. This 'inner word' can remain an 'unmediated experience of the mystery of love' (*M*, 113), real but unrecognised. This orientation to mystery needs to become concrete in the world of meaning. And this happens most of all through Jesus Christ. Lonergan offers the example of a man and woman who love each other but have not yet expressed it to one another. 'Their very silence means that their love has not reached the point of self-surrender' and self-giving (*M*, 113). A new stage in their relationship is born when they reveal their love mutually and explicitly. Likewise a whole new situation arrives with the Word of revelation.

An affective conversion

In this light Lonergan offers his pithy and memorable description of faith as 'the knowledge born of religious love' (*M*, 115). Here he is expressing in more contemporary and more personal language a key insight of Aquinas, who spoke of faith as an act of the intellect commanded by the will. Going further than Aquinas, Lonergan locates this recognition as the summit of a long adventure of human self-transcendence, where the burden of achieving gives way to the surprise of receiving, and, as already seen, to the overwhelming surprise of being loved by God. To know this with mind and heart is faith.

Slowly Lonergan came to see the importance of an 'affective conversion' as central to faith (*3C*, 179). Through a transformation of our feelings, and not just of our ideas, we come to embrace love as God's gift, and so we enter a state of being-in-love. 'Since faith gives more truth than understanding comprehends ... [our] sensitivity needs symbols that unlock its transforming dynamism' (*I*, 744). For the Christian, the image that touches hearts and reveals our lasting source of love is simply the person of Christ. 'Christianity involves not only the inward gift of being in love with God but also the outward expression of God's love in Christ Jesus dying and rising again' (*PGT*, 170).

In this light all our deciding can have a different foundation and tone. 'Desire turns to joy when religious conversion transforms the existential subject into a subject in love, a subject held, grasped, possessed, owned through a total and so an other-worldly love' (*M*, 242). Lonergan, however, wants to describe how faith fits into a map of our human liberation in today's cultural context. He highlights how the upward movement of our self-transcendence is crowned and embraced by the transforming downward movement of God's gift. When we enter this horizon of faith we can reread that upward human journey, and see that it was already being shaped by the quiet artistry of the Spirit, preparing us for the Word that is Christ.

In one of his more eloquent moments Lonergan evokes the religious experience of love in these words:

> It is as though a room were filled with music though one can have no sure knowledge of its source. There is in the world, as it were, a charged field of love and meaning; here and there it reaches a notable intensity; but it is ever unobtrusive, hidden, inviting each of us to join. And join we must if we are to perceive it, for our perceiving is through our own loving (*M*, 290).

The music, like the outpouring of God's love, is everywhere, with varying levels of felt presence. Sometimes overwhelming, sometimes seemingly shy, it surrounds us, inviting us to share in the harmony. Faith is our perception of this symphony of God's own love, a perception that becomes possible only through entering the flow of that music.

In the voice of Lonergan (an imaginary monologue)

At its simplest I see faith as our response to a love that fulfils all our human longing. When God's surprising love is recognised, everything changes. The landscape of life is transformed forever. No doubt the intensity of the first moment, like the intensity of falling in love, will fade. But something else takes over – a being-in-love, an existence that is bathed in the light of being loved by God.

Overcoming blockages

So faith involves a sense of astonishment and of completion. Astonishment, because it goes beyond all our imagining. Completion, because it crowns our searching for meaning and fullness of life. In this way faith is the goal of a necessary and risky human journey. It is necessary because we have to grow up, to go beyond childhood things, as St Paul says, and to enter the kingdom of our freedom. It is risky because, as in so many adventure stories, there are difficulties to be overcome or enemies to be avoided. There are purifying stages before we can come into the light. We need to emerge from the distortions of our culture before we can open to the possibility of love-as-gift. Otherwise we suffer from a narrowness of imagination, where the explosion of transforming love cannot happen. If the real is equated with the visible, then the invisible becomes culturally incredible. So theology has to undertake a therapeutic mission before it can speak worthily of faith and God. At the heart of theology is prayer and in our culture prayer is a rebellion against our addiction to externals, a relaxing into another logic of gift.

Why this emphasis on battlegrounds? We have inherited from modernity not only magnificent achievements but also a shrunken agenda about our roads to truth. It has become difficult to make sense of faith within the dominant philosophical assumptions coming from Descartes or Kant or Marx. They leave us confused about both objectivity and subjectivity. Objectivity was identified with tangible things examinable 'out there'. Subjectivity retreated into inner feelings and intuitions. So there was a deep divorce between two worlds: the world of outer realities and that of the individual self. We have all suffered from this separation. I tried to learn from Aquinas and Newman and other great thinkers how to meet this challenge – not simply by retreating into or repeating the past, but by trying to translate the wisdom of the centuries for the problems of today. Eventually I came to a paradoxical discovery: 'genuine objectivity is the fruit of authentic subjectivity' (*M*, 292). In other words, we arrive at truth through fidelity to a ladder of imperatives present in our ordinary, self-transcending questions. That ladder can be expressed briefly in this way: be attentive (to experience in all its forms); be intelligent (seeking to understanding); be reasonable (checking out the truth); be responsible (making decisions in tune with your knowledge); be in love (because that is the pinnacle of your journey, where faith is born from recognising God's love of you).

Loved into love

That final point is the key. Ultimately it is love that pulls you out of your little self. It liberates you from the prison of merely practical living. When you allow love to hit you (almost like Cupid's arrow), your vision of life expands into consolation. Until that point, it is an uphill struggle to be faithful to the light that you see. You do your best to understand correctly and to choose generously. But it can be a lonely and winding road. Without a clear goal, it is easy to lose your way, or to wander around aimlessly, trying one experience after another without any lasting satisfaction. But when love enters your life, the heart discovers a wavelength of knowing that carries you beyond what the mind can know. Now you are loved into love. You are called both out of yourself and into yourself. This powerful threshold, where love takes over, is always a gift. It is never your achievement, even though it crowns all your efforts to make sense or to follow your conscience. In ways it under-mines all that you imagined before, because this being-in-love becomes a different measure for everything.

All that I have said about love can be true of human loving and also of the love poured into our hearts by God's loving of us. Quite simply, love is the revolution, the most powerful force for transforming our life. And faith is the acknowledg-ment of that gift. I think this can happen in many ways in human life. For instance, when I had three difficult operations for lung cancer at the age of 61, the love of a religious sister, who nursed me back to health, was crucial in restoring my will to live. My experience of receiving such love, and of accepting it, helped me to feel more powerfully what I had always believed about God's love. In ways that my great mentor Newman would call real, and not only notional, I experienced how love can change the horizon of life. It can transform the tone of how we think and imagine and live out our daily choices. So what many people encounter in mutual human loving is our best path towards understanding faith as our conversion to God's love. This blessing of being liberated into a fuller aliveness is what we call grace and it can be experienced in numerous ways in each person's story.

St Augustine once commented, with striking simplicity, that what he wanted to say will be understood only by a person in love. Without that foundation all the apparatus of religion can remain empty or illusory and even dangerous. The wonder of my heart needs food, especially the ordinary flow of daily generosity, received and returned. Dante loved Beatrice and then was ready to celebrate a divine comedy. When the door of love opens, the gaze of the heart learns to interpret everything differently. Love in this sense is a transfigured disposition rather than a transitory feeling.

All this is the blessing of the Spirit rather than our attainment. It is beyond our striving because it involves an experience of surprise, of being invited beyond all our choosing and desiring. To repeat myself: when the gift of love is recognised as coming from God, the response is what we call religious faith.

Beyond beliefs – a new music

A word of caution. To my way of thinking it is not helpful to identify faith with religious beliefs. Even in our ordinary way of speaking about religion, we tend to stress the content of our beliefs. An 'unbeliever' is thought of as someone who does not accept the existence of God, or who rejects the teachings of the Church. But this is to put the cart before the horse. The theatre of faith lies in our affectivity. Without some transforming moment where we recognise that we are loved, we are not talking about Christian faith in its fullness. 'He loved me and gave himself for me', writes St Paul to the Galatians. To grasp that reality is not an intellectual matter but an awakening of heart and imagination to a new relationship.

Obviously we use the word 'love' so easily today that it can lose its power to cause an earthquake in our lives. We know the simple and central words of St John: God is love. To ponder that statement prayerfully causes a constant revolution not only in my images of God but in my whole vision of life. Love is what God is and does, without limits, without conditions. Love is what God is doing all the time, whether we know it or not – like a sculptor releasing a beauty hidden in stone. That love is the ocean in which our lives move. It is the source of our own movement towards a light beyond us. And, to change metaphor, when we begin to hear that overwhelming music of love, inviting us to join, all becomes harmony.

But that love of God for us comes first – as a divine initiative (St John again). Our recognition-response is always an echo, a grateful yes, bathed in wonder. So the creative work of God is to love us into being able to love in a new way. What a relief! Religion can often seem like a difficult command from on high. Instead at its core it is a gift of God's own love poured into our hearts, to heal our hope, raise our sights, and set free our loving. Genuine religion is about this liberation of hearts and energies, not as a theory but as a daily adventure of fullness. As I said, the final imperative of our authenticity is simple: be in love. Not in the sense of a distant command, but as a joyful embrace of a gift. And when we know that gift, especially when we encounter it in Christ, what we call faith is born. In Christ, I glimpse, with graced ease, a door open into the mystery of God as Trinity. So faith is a relational knowing which brings about a radical change in how we live our freedom. Here our long adventure of self-transcendence discovers a ladder of ordinary ecstasy. Self-belonging is transformed by belonging to the Lord. Faith thus becomes the hinge of our existence, not simply a vague belief in God, or some routine gesture of religiousness. It is a new space where God's out-poured love has reached us.

As we look back on our lives, from this new perspective, we see that all our genuine moments of self-transcendence were religious without our realising it at the time. In the whole outward and upward movement of our hearts God was active. But when we come to recognise this, and to speak to the Artist of our love in prayer, a new situation comes to birth. 'This complete being-in-love ... is the reason of the heart that reason does not know' (2C, 129). It is the eye of faith that sees everything differently, life and death, joy and tragedy, the struggles of history: all is now the theatre of God's call and companionship.

Here, the Magnificat becomes magnificently true. God has done great things, meeting our deepest hungers. All is God's doing. We walk in the flow of divine creativity, even when we think it is all our doing. God's promise is received and fulfilled in the slowness of our daily learning. At the peak of our freedom the music changes: it is no longer our effort that counts but our yes of recognition, of gratitude, and of an authenticity that is not ours. Yes, faith, born from love and giving birth to love, is the God-intended crown of our long journey towards a fullness for here and hereafter.

References to works of Bernard Lonergan

C = Collection, ed. F. Crowe and R. Doran, Toronto, 1988.

2C = A Second Collection, ed. W. Ryan and B. Tyrrell, London, 1974.

3C = A Third Collection, ed. F. Crowe, London, 1985.

I = Insight: A Study of Human Understanding, ed. F. Crowe and R. Doran, Toronto, 1992.

M = Method in Theology, London, 1972.

PGT = 'Philosophy of God and Theology' (3 lectures) in *Philosophical and Theological Papers 1965–1980*, ed. R. Croken and R. Doran, Toronto, 2004.

6

Flannery O'Connor: assaulting the imagination

In all probability, Flannery O'Connor would be both surprised and pleased to find herself appearing in a book of this kind. When she died of lupus in 1964 at the age of thirty-nine, she was already well known, and even controversial, as a Catholic writer of fiction. If her style of drastic distortion, or Southern Grotesque, as she sometimes described it, left some people confused or even stunned, that was just the impact she wanted. Faith for her often meant an upheaval or rupture with what we take for granted about ourselves or about religion.

Her fame has soared in the decades since her death. Thomas Merton saw her as an equal of Sophocles. More than seventy books have been written on her work. When her essays and letters were published, they showed her to be the most theologically alert novelist of the entire century. She called herself a 'hillbilly Thomist' who read Aquinas for twenty minutes every night before going to bed. On this point something of her ironic spirit is seen in a letter of 1955 (imitating the style of the *Summa*):

> If my mother were to come in during this process and say, 'Turn off the light. It's late,' I with lifted finger and broad bland beatific expression, would reply, 'On the contrary, I answer that the light, being eternal and limitless, cannot be turned off. Shut your eyes.' (*HB*, 93–4.)

Her theological horizon was further nourished during the last eight years of her life, when she wrote short reviews of at least a hundred religious books for local Catholic periodicals, thus encountering the works of such figures as Péguy, Maritain, Voege-lin, Guardini, Barth, Teilhard de Chardin, Congar, Vawter, Küng, Durwell, Ong, Edith Stein, William Lynch and von Hügel. She also read various works of such French authors as Mauriac, Mou-nier, Bernanos, Simone Weil, Gilson and Daniélou. 'I read a lot of theology because it makes my writing bolder', she once commented (*BGF*, 228), and on another occasion she added, 'I'm no theologian, but all this is vital to me' (*CW*, 1118). With her combined passion for theology and for religious themes in fiction, undoubtedly she merits her place in a book about faith.

The Irish novelist Brian Moore, himself a declared agnostic, admitted that he had disliked Flannery O'Connor's stories until one day when he picked up her large volume of letters, *The Habit of Being*, and realised the richly ironic spirit in which her fiction was written. Her narrative style is at once tongue-in-cheek in its accumulation of mocking details, and yet deadly serious in its scope to embody encounters with grace. She was dismissive about a Catholic tendency for instant answers and hence a divorce of reason from imagination. These reductive approaches will be healed only 'if we realize that faith is a "walking in darkness" and not a theological solution to mystery'. In this sense she wanted her fiction to lead readers towards such 'deeper and stranger visions' (*MM*, 184).

In fact she remarked that, judging from the letters she received, prisoners seemed to understand her best, because they knew something about destructiveness and conflict. In her life, too, she knew plenty about struggles and shadows, especially through her long battle with sickness. From her mid-twenties she was aware of the possibility of an early death, and no doubt it gave urgency to her tone. Her letters never display any self-pity on this score and she expressed impatience with those who thought her writing was handicapped by her illness. 'I write with my head, not my feet', she told one interviewer who asked about her crutches. Less than a month before she died she wrote to a religious sister (with word play on her illness): 'The wolf, I'm afraid, is inside tearing up the place ... I count on your prayers' (*HB*, 591).

Shock strategy

O'Connor's horizon offers a useful foil to the more academic authors explored in other chapters here. She dramatises again and again the costly transformation of vision that faith entails and the subterfuges we use for escaping its more demanding aspects. She told of one lady in California, who complained that the stories did

not lift her heart when she came home tired. O'Connor commented shrewdly that 'if her heart had been in the right place, it
would have been lifted up' (*MM*, 48). She goes on to say that when
our sense of evil is diluted, we easily forget 'the price of restoration'
(*MM*, 48). T. S. Eliot recognised her 'uncanny talent' but some
stories 'horrified' him and his nerves could not 'take much of a
disturbance' (*BGF*, 272). O'Connor would have been happy with
this reaction: 'you have to push as hard as the age that pushes
against you' (*HB*, 229). When the surrounding culture does not
share your Christian faith, 'then you have to make your vision
apparent by shock – to the hard of hearing you shout, and for the
almost blind you draw large and startling figures' (*CW*, 805–806).
Thus the wit of her fiction was often aimed at the defence mecha-
nisms of a secular culture, or indeed of cock-sure religiousness. The
novelist John Hawkes described her attitude to life as full of energy,
detachment, pleasure and grace, and because of this her writings
could be wry, brutal and comic. She would probably have identified
with this provocative statement from another novelist, Georges
Bernanos: 'The modern world needs to hear a few liberating voices,
but the voices that set us free are not the tranquillizing, reassuring
ones'.

   In July 1955 O'Connor was delighted to get a letter from a
certain Betty Hester who recognised that her stories were mainly
about God. She wrote back (in the first of what was to be a series of
nearly 200 letters) saying, 'I am a Catholic peculiarly possessed of
the modern consciousness' (*CW*, 942). In a second letter to Hester
two weeks later she added that for her 'there is only one Reality',
the Incarnation in which 'nobody believes' today, and hence 'my
audience are the people who think God is dead' (*CW*, 943). In one
of her lectures she put it more strongly: 'Redemption is meaning-
less unless there is cause for it in the actual life we live, and for the
last few centuries there has been operating in our culture the
secular belief that there is no such cause' (*CW*, 805).

Incarnational prophet

In this way, O'Connor set out to disturb the complacency of both
agnostics and over-secure believers, and she did so through a

certain extremism of style and plot. She scorned any form of didactic religious fiction, describing a novel by Cardinal Spellman as useful 'as a doorstop' but not helping the standards of Catholic literature (*MM*, 175). Similarly she hated 'pious language' because, as she wrote to an unbelieving friend, 'I believe the realities it hides' (*CW*, 1035). Her language had to be down to earth, showing rather than telling (to echo a distinction she borrowed from Henry James). Therefore an 'incarnational art', she argued, should never become detached from a 'dramatic sense' of the concrete (*MM*, 68, 146–7). A Christian novelist moves in a 'larger universe' than mere naturalism, because 'the natural world contains the supernatural' (*MM*, 175). It was never a question of climbing out of the narrative into its meaning, because a good story resists paraphrase: instead 'it hangs on and expands in the mind' (*MM*, 108). She chose to recount tales of fundamentalist figures of the Bible Belt, ranging from characters of ferocious faith to others of fierce atheism. Rooted in credible and often comic externals, her hope was to push her plot and her readers 'towards mystery and the unexpected' (*MM*, 44), because 'mystery is a great embarrassment to the modern mind', and, in her view, often eliminated by education.

O'Connor's path towards faith meant going through the surfaces of life towards the shock of strangeness. She came to define this approach as prophetic and recounted in various letters her lucky discovery that Aquinas held that 'prophetic vision is a quality of the imagination' (*CW*, 1116) and that 'prophetic vision is dependent on the imagination of the prophet' (and not on any moral quality). She came to hold that enlarging people's imagination was a key role for the Church and for a Catholic writer of fiction. Her stories wanted to serve faith by showing imagination being challenged and changed in her characters, and at the same time leading her readers towards a larger vision of reality. 'The prophet is a realist of distances', in the sense of 'seeing far things close up' and things near at hand 'with their extensions of meaning' (*MM*, 44). This prophetic realism was embodied in some of her characters as well as in her fictional method. 'It is a realism which does not hesitate to distort appearances in order to show a hidden truth' (*MM*, 179). And the hidden truth nearly always involves an amazing grace, not as a soft music but as a divine explosion. On this disturbing transformation she pulled no punches: 'I don't know if anyone can be converted without seeing themselves in a blasting annihilating light, a blast that will last a lifetime' (*HB*, 427). I am reminded of a saying of Sebastian Moore that the Gospel 'is life meeting its obstacle in us and exploding'.

O'Connor was a rooted and proudly orthodox Catholic, but she was not slow to point out and even satirise the human warts of the Church. 'Ideal Christianity doesn't exist' (*CW*, 1182). Although many of her characters come from low-church traditions, she commented that 'Smugness is the Great Catholic Sin. I find it in myself' (*CW*, 983). People who know 'only the Jansenist-Mechanical Catholic' are right to be put off: this mindset represents not 'faith but a kind of false certainty', and in place of 'the body of Christ' it puts a 'poor man's insurance system' (*CW*, 1037–8). These 'unimaginative and half-dead Catholics' would be 'startled to know' the full richness of the tradition they cling to with a kind of blind loyalism (*CW*, 1118).

If she attacked superficial Church belonging, she remained a great defender of a genuinely Church-grounded faith. Without any 'real imaginative vision of what the Church is', she told her friend Cecil Dawkins in 1959, it is easy to reject a sociological image of it, not realising that 'dogma is the guardian of mystery' (*CW*, 1115–16). Most discussions of religion seemed to be ignorant, superficial and unworthy of the true nature of the issues. Without a 'larger imaginative view' one cannot be 'alive to spiritual reality' (*CW*, 1117). If her writing was to be truly prophetic, it had to find ways of awakening that spiritual imagination wavelength, of making the realities of Incarnation and Redemption dramatically real, and hence of suggesting the seriousness of any faith option.

The impact of grace

O'Connor seems more interested in pre-evangelisation than in more direct communication of the Gospel (although she would dislike this jargon). Her narratives work indirectly to provoke an awakening to religious possibilities, instead of communicating the creedal content of faith. What she remarked of one story can be more widely applied: 'It's not so much a story of conversion as of self-knowledge, which I suppose has to be the first step in conversion' (*CW*, 1076). Part of the rhetoric of her fiction is to enlarge the reader's self-awareness, even if she has to use shock tactics. In the same letter she spoke about the 'religious sense' being deadened when doctrines are reduced to human proportions in order to explain them away: as a result 'there is no sense of the power of God that could produce the Incarnation and the Resurrection' (*CW*, 1077). Therefore her hope was to change the disposition of her readers, by jolting them out of their securities and towards some imaginative openness to religious experience.

In this sense her stories often hinge on moments of grace that are not just surprising but sometimes violent. 'It seems to me that all good stories are about conversion, about a character's changing ... The action of grace changes a character' (*CW*, 1067). She stressed the conflictual nature of an encounter with grace, and how, if readers do not appreciate this, they dismiss her stories as merely pessimistic: 'All my stories are about the action of grace on a character who is not very willing to support it, but most people think of these stories as hard, hopeless, brutal' (*CW*, 1067). She had little time for people who thought of religion as meeting their own felt needs and so there is often a hard edge to her picture of faith: 'truth does not change according to our ability to stomach it emotionally'; on the contrary faith can be 'emotionally disturbing, downright repulsive' as in the darker experiences of saints (*CW*, 952). Faith, in her view, often causes upheaval before it can experience the fruits of joy. She does not seem to have known the Spiritual Exercises of Ignatius of Loyola, but she would have appreciated his metaphor that grace enters a receptive spirit like water gently into a sponge, but in the case of someone closed in egoism it is like water falling more noisily on a stone. Her stories are narrative dynamite to break open that stone. As one of her early commentators said, she undermines our rationalism but you don't realise it until afterwards.

After her death *Time* magazine was partly right in its comment that she 'wrote exclusively of ultimate things'. It is true that her stories often depict people arriving unexpectedly at moments of death or judgement, and it is equally true that she presents these realities with a starkness that is intended to shake people's self-satisfaction. She was struck by this sentence from Emmanuel Mounier: 'Love is a struggle: life is a struggle against death' (*BGF*, 308). She must have had her own daily sense of mortality and yet her fiction is never directly about herself. She transformed her own shadows into stories that were comic, incarnational and never moralistic. The version of faith she presents can seem austere, but her narratives of ferocious humour often point to more joyful discoveries. They are also born from a real solidarity and compassion for agonised unbelievers. In a letter dated 1959 she wrote: 'I think there is no suffering greater than what is caused by the doubts of those who want to believe. I know what torment this is, but I can only see it, in myself anyway, as the process by which faith is deepened' (*CW*, 1110).

Two conversion stories

Rich though they are, O'Connor's non-fictional writings do not give us her fullest light on the drama of faith. I have chosen two of her stories to represent the irruption of grace in the lives of two women who suffer from a 'distorted sense of spiritual purpose' (*MM*, 32). Both of them share a certain proud security about their own way of living, including their version of Christian faith. They are figures of comic rigidity, accustomed to domineering over those around them. Both narratives, with an evocative style full of details, lead the central characters and the readers, to a climax of new vision. The 'grotesque' plots bring us through purgatory towards some kind of paradise. They lead to climactic confrontations with invisible mystery.

'Revelation', O'Connor's favourite story completed in the last winter of her life, traces the awakening of Mrs Turpin to her own hypocrisy as a Christian and ultimately to the differentness of God. Two revelations therefore, one humiliating, and the other like a hymn of joy. Located in totally concrete settings, a doctor's waiting room and later a pig farm, her complacency undergoes a double therapy. At one moment in the waiting room (perhaps itself a comic symbol) Mrs Turpin is crowing out to everyone her thanks to Jesus for having 'a little of everything, and a good disposition besides' (*CW*, 644). At this point a disturbed girl, called Mary Grace (!), flings a book (called *Human Development*) at her eye and then calls her a warthog from hell. This first dent in her armour fuels a rage against God on the part of Mrs Turpin, and that evening she finds herself roaring at God across the pigs. Scriptural echoes of Jacob and of the Prodigal Son are probably deliberate, but the main plot is the conversion of a Pharisee. 'Who do you think you are?', she yells at God. But ironically her question returns as an echo, which is 'like an answer from beyond the wood'. Mrs Turpin remains transfixed, gazing 'at the very heart of mystery' in the pig pen, 'as if she were absorbing some abysmal life-giving knowledge'. The story ends with her vision of a procession of hordes of people she had despised 'rumbling toward heaven', while her own type of respectable believers march with dignity at the end. 'She could see by their shocked and altered faces that even their virtues were being burned away'. As she walks home by a 'darkening path', she can still hear 'the voices of the souls climbing upward into the starry field and shouting hallelujah' (*CW*, 653–4).

Even from a selective summary of this kind, it is clear that O'Connor's faith map takes us through a painful erosion of the ego before allowing us a more consoling image of salvation. Her method is concrete, hilarious, but rooted in a rich theology. We may need to be shaken out of our religious securities before we can glimpse that second revelation of God's greatness. In less dramatic ways than the case of Mrs Turpin, our sense of God can itself become a comfortable and comforting crutch. O'Connor wants to push us through rough terrains of self-knowledge, preparing the way for a God who is always greater – and more ambitious – than we might like.

Thresholds of mystery

Something of the same pattern can be found in 'A Good Man is Hard to Find', an earlier story that O'Connor often chose when invited to read or perform one of her texts. The story tells of a family outing that passes through territory where a dangerous bandit called the Misfit is on the loose. The machinations of the Grandmother cause them to fall into his hands and worse still, she seals their fate by recognising him. When all the family are taken off to be shot by his henchmen, the Grandmother remains alone with him, only to undergo a surprising moment of grace, which is at once comic, serious and even terrible. One of O'Connor's own comments offers a good light on this episode: 'it is the extreme situation that best reveals what we are essentially' (*MM*, 113).

In keeping with her long life of manipulation, the Grandmother advises the criminal to pray but he rejects any need for help: 'I'm doing all right by myself' (a sentence that sums up a lot of modern atheism). She again tries to talk her way out of danger, telling the Misfit that he is a good man and mentioning Jesus. But this anti-Christ figure shows a greater awareness of Jesus than she does: the Resurrection has 'thrown everything off balance'. If it is all true, you should follow him and give up everything; if not, there is 'no pleasure but meanness'. His anguish seems to move her to a rare moment of clarity, beyond all her prattling and pretence, and she reaches out to touch him as 'one of my own children'. She had never been closer to real faith in her life and in that instant of her closeness to mystery, he shoots her. His comment to his companion is one of the most famous lines in O'Connor's work: 'She would have been a good woman, if it had been somebody there to shoot her every minute of her life'. And the story ends with a tiny hint of his possible conversion: his last words are that there is 'no real pleasure in life' (*CW*, 152–3). Has something of the Grandmother's last-minute grace touched this sceptical Christ-haunted figure? If so, the pleasure of meanness may not be the only possible road any more.

O'Connor later commented that 'a moment of grace excites the devil to frenzy' (*CW*, 1121), but she also described the story as a duel between the Grandmother's superficial faith 'and the Misfit's more profoundly felt involvement with Christ's action' (*CW*, 1148–9). In O'Connor's vision (and perhaps echoing her own acute sense of mortality), it is on the 'verge of eternity' that faith comes into focus, and in spite of our distorted selves, 'in us the good is something under construction' (*MM*, 114, 226). Faith in O'Connor bursts into enemy territory in sometimes violent ways, as if God has to break down the defences before offering a new and joyful vision. Her favourite prayer, which she said every day for years, was to Saint Raphael as the 'angel of happy meeting'. Less than a month before her death she sent it to a friend. 'Lonely and tired, crushed by the separations and sorrows of life [we ask] that we may not be as strangers in the province of joy … you whose home lies beyond the region of thunder' (*HB*, 592–3).

In the voice of O'Connor (an imaginary monologue)

(This attempt to capture what Flannery O'Connor might say to us on faith today draws mainly on a set of letters she sent to an Emory University student called Alfred Corn. She had given a talk at the university and this young poet wrote to her afterwards partly about her fiction but also saying that he had lost his faith. Between May and August of 1962 Flannery wrote to him four times, letters that express with clarity and humour her wisdom concerning faith. In these pages expressions that come directly from these or other letters will be given in italics. However the object here, as in other chapters of this book, is to imagine, with a certain freedom, what she might say today[1].)

It surprises me when people are surprised that faith is fragile or that it goes through tunnels of trouble. I'm convinced that it is often like a lighthouse, with an alteration of light and dark. So the experience of darkness, of thinking that you have lost your faith *is an experience that in the long run belongs to faith.* Especially in today's context I would say that faith, paradoxically, needs to be grounded in unbelief! Surely the Gospel cry of 'Lord, I believe, Help my unbelief' is *the most natural and most human and most agonizing prayer in the Gospels.* It captures the pendulum experience between trust and panic that is our ordinary path in faith, as long as we are in this life of non-seeing and in this modern culture continually *bombarded with new frames of reference.*

There is a common mistake people make about faith, especially when they think that have lost it: they identify it with knowledge and forget that it involves doing as well.

---

1   The letters to Corn can be found in Flannery O'Connor, *The Habit of Being*, New York, 1979, 476–89; or in Flannery O'Connor, *Collected Works*, The Library of America, New York, 1988, 1163–74.

Remember the Gospel saying, whoever does the truth comes into the light. That brings us back to a richer version of truth than our usual one. Truth of any important kind can never be a head thing alone. Truth is to be done in the sense of to be lived. I recall a surprising answer that the Jesuit poet Hopkins gave to his agnostic friend Robert Bridges, who had written asking how he might make sense of faith. When perhaps *he expected a long philosophical answer, Hopkins wrote back, 'Give alms'.* In other words, God is experienced most of all in acts of love. But we can get *so entangled with intellectual difficulties* that we forget this simpler and perhaps harder road, not of thinking but of self-giving. *Faith is what you have in the absence of knowledge* and its surest nourishment lies in how you live your life. But I am *no vague believer.* I cling to the definiteness both of Christ and of the Church. Strangely we need doctrines to protect the mystery of faith which is beyond all our words.

So the long adventure of being a believer, especially nowadays, requires a lot of self-patience. When one difficulty is overcome, another comes along. At one moment you will have difficulties with the human weakness, or even the scandalous sinfulness, of the Church. You work your way to some wise sense of history on this issue only to run into the plurality of world religions. Is there no stability or security for faith? *Where you have absolute solutions, you have no need for faith.* As the years pass I am more and more rooted in my Catholicism, and yet more and more reticent about easy clarities about God. *How incomprehensible God must necessarily be to be the God of heaven and earth. You can't fit the Almighty into your intellectual categories.*

Stretching the imagination

Besides, one's life of faith is always on the move, or at least it should be. God's Spirit in you will keep you growing and changing, if you allow Him or Her to do so. Not towards some comfortable certainty that never impacts on life but towards a self-losing that is a liberation for love. Often the life-style around us causes *a shrinking of the imaginative life* but the

Spirit continues to invite us into new spaces through *a stretch-ing of the imagination*. Once again the mind or intellect is not the main friend of faith. I have great respect for the intellect but not as a solo act. It needs its family around it to flourish. It needs Sister Imagination and Brother Will and above all Mother Gift. *Yes, faith is a gift, but the will has a great deal to do with it.*

To lose faith, which we say as if it were like a handkerchief, is really a failure of desire, but ably *assisted by sterile intellect*. The genuine intellect is far from sterile because it helps us to see the beauty of truth. *God has given us reason to use and it can lead us towards a knowledge of God, though analogy.* Analogy connects up with the rest of life, where intellect walks hand in hand with desire, imagination, prayerfulness, and all our gradual alteration through being loved by God and learn-ing to love a little. It is very simple really: *it is reasonable to believe, even though these beliefs are beyond reason.* And yet that 'beyond' can seem very strange because it pushes us towards newness. Faith is not simply *a big electric blanket*. We move kicking and screaming into new freedom because the old and smaller places seem safer, and certainly less costly.

I don't for a moment deny that faith brings consolation, even at times strongly felt joy. But it does not depend on your feelings. The presence or absence of faith cannot be measured by how you feel. Faith is true independently of whether it gives you *security and emotional release*. There is a flabby sort of religious experience much sought after today, which *depends on feeling instead of thought*, and which turns *religion into poetry and therapy*. I have no time for such liberal wooliness. It's like saying that *grace before meals is an aid to digestion*! The God I believe in has the power to take me out of my inner poverty into an amazing call and a promise that points to eternity. My faith is grounded in Christ's revelation and history. It is verified, I believe, by the tradition of the church and especially by the saints (verify literally means 'made-true-by-doing'). Feelings of fullness are a blessing when they come our way, but to focus on them alone risks making faith *our own sweet invention*. Faith is God's business but recognised (or not) by us. Of course the most concrete foundation for faith is

Jesus Christ, and *if Christ wasn't God he was merely pathetic, not beautiful.*

A complex freedom

I have been attacking a few familiar illusions and idols. That faith is meant to stay still. That it basks steadily in the sunshine of certainty. That with faith you can expect to feel near to God all the time. That intellect, especially the kind of detached intellect in fashion today, is the only criterion of truth. That faith should be without struggle or crisis. *Let me tell you this: faith rises and falls like the tides of an invisible ocean. If it is as presumptuous to think that faith will stay with you forever, it is just as presumptuous to think that unbelief will.* So be ready for a rocky road, whether you are a believer or not. The road will lose its rockiness only when you stop your honest searching, or else opt for the centrality of your own self. That last situation is a real trap. *Some people when they lose their faith in Christ, substitute a swollen faith in themselves.* That inflated ego was a frequent starting point in my stories, as I tried to explore the comedy and the tragedy of our many forms of original pride, and then its painful erosion by grace. Our freedom is never simple, and my comic approach to seriousness is meant to capture that mystery of ourselves.

Perhaps I should qualify one of my earlier points. I tend to state things too strongly, a temperamental temptation of a writer of 'grotesque' stories. Faith cannot depend on feelings but feelings are important. In some of my stories, for instance at the end of 'Revelation' or 'The Artificial Nigger', people are taken out of themselves by an overwhelming sense of awe and fullness, in a way that crowns the healing of their distorted egos. Sometimes we are blessed with such consolation. No doubt we should occasionally ask for the fog to lift and for light to shine in our hearts. But it is God's doing, when and if God sees fit. Faith is strengthened by these experiences of grace but normally it has to walk without much light. That is where my trust in church tradition comes in. It keeps my faith strugglingly alive, when my feelings about God are blank, confused, or downright negative. Those roots give me steadiness because I rely on something bigger than my own solitary self. Ultimately *if you admit redemption, you are no pessimist.* When people don't even recognise their self-prisons, I try to expose their unreadiness for grace. But thankfully we are not alone. More important is God's readiness to find a chink in our armour and to change our vision in ways that we could never imagine for ourselves. Ultimately faith reveals how valuable we are, because our life, in spite of everything, was *found by God to be worth dying for.*

References to works of Flannery O'Connor

BGF = Brad Gooch, *Flannery: a life of Flannery O'Connor*, New York, 2009.

CW = Flannery O'Connor, *Collected Works*, New York, 1988.

HB = *The Habit of Being: Letters of Flannery O'Connor*, ed. Sally Fitzgerald, New York, 1979.

MM = *Mystery and Manners: Occasional Prose*, ed. Sally & Robert Fitzgerald, London, 1972.

7

Dorothee Soelle: mystical–activist faith

Dorothee Soelle's faith map is needed in this book. Without the dimension of justice that she voices, and the theology of mystical resistance that she proposes, the picture of faith could remain lopsidedly personal and spiritual. Without the contact with suffering that she narrates, our God-talk could remain insulated from the wounded world all around us, and our image of faith would lack social grit. When Moses was called by God at the burning bush, that encounter was not just to strengthen his personal faith. It was because God had heard the cry of oppressed people and wanted to send them a liberator. Soelle brought this biblical moment up to date, putting it in contact with contemporary questions. Although she was personally involved in the liberation theology of Latin America and elsewhere, she saw herself as called to challenge the more comfortable Western world, first in her native Germany and later in the United States. Her fear was that Christianity today, including her own Lutheran tradition, could become 'the religion of the rich' in the sense of a 'suffering-free religion for a world perceived as without suffering' (S, 128).

Overcoming apathy

Even this initial summary introduces a note in the chord of faith that has not been strongly heard in previous chapters in this book. At one point, Balthasar was described as a 'dialectical' theologian. The same would be true of Soelle, except that her stance was very different (and she would probably criticise Balthasar for being rather too 'timeless' in his theology). Her starting point for theology is not biblical revelation but our contemporary situation of 'estrangement' or alienation. This is a form of cultural sin, which she describes as 'being cut off from life' (CL, 22). Like other dialectical thinkers, she highlights the crucial role of choice, of taking a stand, but she extends this beyond merely in existential horizons. Hers is a more political, activist and ᵣ... stand.

The conflict she sees between the Gospel and the world stems from the ills that dominate our culture, ranging from violence to indifference. The phenomenon of apathy is a special target of Soelle's criticism. Literally the term implies an inability to suffer but she enlarges to include an incapacity for compassion. In her view, a socially induced apathy leaves people separate from each other, crippled in conscience, and blind to their complicity in the unjust divisions of our planet. Apathy becomes, in Soelle's theology, the principal enemy of faith. 'The apathetic God is not the God of the little people and their pain' (*S*, 101). If even God is beyond suffering, as often depicted, that God is incredible. If people are shielded from the suffering of others, God becomes unreal and unnecessary in their lives. An image of apathy in God produces distance and numbness in believers.

If one reads the surrounding culture in this light, faith entails a passionate 'struggle against objective and subjective cynicism' (*CL*, 15). It stands not only for transcendence but for radical change. A sense of impotence leaves people without hope, but rooted in the liberating Word of God, we can see through oppressive systems and overcome temptations to inaction. In the Gospels the opposite of faith is fear and in today context 'faith means fighting against the prevailing cynicism and standing up to it' (*CL*, 11). It implies 'choosing life', to cite the title of one of her books. Like many theologians of the late twentieth century, Soelle has moved the agenda of faith from the zone of truth to that of freedom. In her case freedom is not just an inner quality of the self but an active quality that can resist a consumerist dictatorship and create alternative embodiments of the Christian living. Her proposal is for an 'exodus theology' with a focus on Christ as liberator (*CL*, 48).

Critique of individualist religion

If the life-style of the dominant culture induces indifference, an individualist religion simply collaborates with this shrinking of hopes. Soelle directs her critique against the reduction of Christianity to narrowly personal horizons. We have inherited, she says, a form of bourgeois religion that stifles the real power of the Gospel. If, in addition, God is seen as separate from human life, faith is in even deeper trouble. In brief, the enemies to faith that she identifies are not in some realm of philosophical ideas: the real enemies are the social, cultural and political situations that blinker people's capacity to see. A God divorced from reality sits easily with individuals who remain cushioned from the struggles of the poor.

Describing herself as 'a German after Auschwitz', Soelle recounts how she herself gradually emerged from a 'liberal' model of thinking in order to see that she had been born into a 'collective estrangement' (*CL*, 40). She needed to grow into a shared remembering and a shared sense of responsibility rather than a merely individualist one. Thus sin came to be understood not simply as individual failure but as participation in social structures of evil. In this spirit she paraphrases St Paul, with a deliberate change of vocabulary: 'The system of injustice shall no longer determine the way you live, so that you run after false dreams' (*CL*, 29, adapting Rom. 6:12).

Common in Protestant spirituality, she comments, is the saying that everyone is alone with his or her God; but this focus on the isolated self can link up with a sense of the Cross as simply a 'cry of loneliness' thus robbing it 'of its political dimension' (*CL*, 54). Such tendencies foster a spiritualising or romanticising of the Gospel. 'We related the cross to the bearing of individual suffering. We cut it off from struggle. Indeed we didn't even see the crosses that stood round about us' (*CL*, 81).

In her emerging vision, Christian faith calls us into solidarity with suffering through being 'in Christ' here and now. 'More belongs to my identity than my individual existence' (*CL*, 67). In order to be fruitful in today's world, faith has to break the stranglehold of individualism, unmask any lazy neutrality, and arrive at a new 'relationality' (*CL*, 69) with Christ and with all of humanity.

Beyond mere theism

Soelle is blunt about her desire to widen the agenda of faith and alter our typical images of God. Because she grew up in Germany in the years immediately after the fall of Nazism, she shared with others of her generation a series of agonising questions about God and Auschwitz. As a young theologian she visited those terrible scenes and experienced a shaking of her Lutheran foundations. It meant a collapse of all the 'omni' attributes of divinity: omnipotence, omniscience, omnipresence. Feeling shame for her country, it became clear to Soelle that a dangerously deformed God had been worshipped by believers who did not actively oppose the Hitler regime. Their Church belonging was narrowly devotional and hence too cosy and unchallenging; or else their image of God was a distant authoritarian father, where divine transcendence had no place for immanence. Their explanation of tragedy depended on the idea that God permits evil, can intervene (rarely) in history, but ultimately is in complete control of everything.

On this last point Soelle comments, with her typical literary flair, that God is not so much an 'interventionist' as an 'intentionist' who 'makes the divine will and intention discernible. I could simply say: God dreams us, even today ... I grasped that God needs us in order to realise what was intended in creation. God dreams us and we should not let God dream alone' (*TS*, 16).

Frequently Soelle expressed her impatience with the traditional question: do you believe in God? In this typical expression she suspected an underlying image of God as a powerful Supreme Being alien from human realities. She quoted Luther: 'You believe in God? You do well. So does the devil' (*TG*, 172), and in this spirit she too attacked a merely theistic reduction of faith. A more valid question would be: 'do you live out God?' (*TG*, 186), implying that authentic faith is not simply an affirmation of God's existence, but rather an event-encounter ('God happens'), which calls us to a transformation of self and of world. Faith as a relationship involves 'bearing witness to God in a world dominated by death' (*TG*, 172).

She came to reject traditional theism as naïve and as unworthy both of human experience and of Christian revelation. This God was too remote, too transcendent, too philosophical, and hence incapable of meeting the human experience of suffering. This God was an 'it', reduced to an object like other objects, not really a 'Thou', not a God to be prayed to, to whom one could cry out like the Psalmists. Such theism talks always of God and never of Jesus:

indeed much atheism arises from 'a theism that has almost nothing to do with Christ' (*S*, 143). In place of all these inadequate images, Soelle insisted on God as 'radical immanence', to be encountered within the drama of human transformation and not 'out there above us all'. She sought to re-imagine faith more in terms of relationship than of power. Faith, in her view, needed to find nourishment in a new and threefold convergence: by bringing together mysticism, solidarity those who suffer, and poetic expressions of prayerfulness.

If she had little time for a cold theodicy, she also rejected the tendency of some Christians to glorify suffering as inevitable and to foster an attitude of mere submission. She stressed that the God revealed through Christ enters into the struggles of history, suffers torture and death, and leads us into the victory of love that is Resurrection. We discover a genuinely 'Christian understanding of suffering' only through 'the mysticism of the cross' (*S*, 101). This does not mean a masochism or cult of pain, nor an image of God as stern pedagogue, teaching us through suffering. Nor does it entail an uninvolved or stoic stance of resignation before injustice. We enter this deeper vision through a double experience: knowing and standing with the poor, and opening ourselves to a mystical path of prayer. 'Mystical love ... transcends every God who is less than love. The concrete expression of such love is not so rare as it might seem. Experience teaches that pain and suffering are in certain situations easily borne' (*S*, 94).

Inner and outer journeys

As already mentioned, Soelle sensed a prevailing superficiality in the emerging post-war world. People's images of their own selves were influenced by the escapist frivolity of the media. She came to diagnose this cultural crisis as the absence of a language for faith, hope or love. This affective wasteland made compassion and prayer impossible. It left people incapable of the Gospel journey of love as implying a dying to themselves. Even the word compassion, as Soelle might say, includes passion, and she was led to a new insight into the connection between mysticism, poetry and passionate activism. To overcome the deadening influence of cultural paralysis would need a marriage of 'inwardness and involvement'; otherwise 'we do not have enough experience to ... speak about religion' (*IR*, 56–57).

The contemplative dimension of Soelle's exploration of faith is also a way of overcoming a utilitarian or merely masculine approach. Without a prayerful and receptive dimension, even militancy for justice could court disillusion or bitterness in the long term. Theological clarities without roots in religious experience put the cart before the horse. There is a 'yearning for something different' that cannot be met by 'prefabricated expressions', but only by prayer experience (*IR*, 128).

Soelle sees a need for two phases in spirituality in order to nourish a mature faith today. The first is an inward journey of silence, self-emptying, and new self-identity through encounter with the mystery of God. Here she draws on the German mystical tradition of Silesius, Eckhart and Suso. They led her to ponder 'the birth of God in the soul' (*IR*, 83) and to the desire to unite oneself with God's action in us. After this inner journey comes a return journey with God – back into the struggles of reality. The full meaning of the mystical is not found in 'absorption into God' but in 'experiences of liberation', where 'solidarity is the most human expression of God's love' (*IR*, 134). Faith communities need both of these movements, if they want to transform a dehumanised and dehumanising culture. 'Praying and struggling' can then 'become once more the breath of a whole culture', especially through small groups of committed Christians.

Dorothee Soelle's final book was a lengthy exploration of 'mysticism and resistance' entitled *The Silent Cry*, published in German in 1997. Here she visited many spiritual figures, in different religions, as witnessing to a transcendence of 'self-imposed and imagined limits' (*SC*, 27). But all of these great mystics, ranging from Teresa of Avila to Dorothy Day, from Simone Weil to Herder Camara, invite us beyond self-realisation in order to resist and transform 'death-oriented reality' (*SC*, 93). This kind of mysticism 'necessarily puts us in radical opposition to what is regarded as a normal way of life' (*SC*, 195). In this perspective faith is healthily disturbing, because it makes people culturally homeless, or unable to buy into the dominant values. And in this book Soelle broadens her concerns to include a care for the planet: the emerging sensibility today reveals our need for 'a different spiritual foundation for the earth's survival and all its inhabitants' (*SC*, 296).

Narrative and poetic languages

Borrowing a saying from the Hassidic tradition, Soelle underlined a danger for Christians in the First World if they become used to living in unrecognised exile: 'we do not look on our life in the affluent society as if we were in Egypt' (*CL*, 1). Insofar as we feel at home under the Pharaoh of contemporary life-styles, we become passive believers incapable of transforming action. If we are kidnapped by consumerism, we may fail to notice the ravages wrought by this soft dictatorship. The poetry of our hearts is smothered even as our social consciousness is put to sleep. Like losing a language, we can be left without genuine expressions for faith. With the cultural air we breathe we accept certain assumptions that are in fact far from the Gospel: that individualism is normal, that the evils around are part of the human condition, and therefore that nothing can be done to change our pained and despairing world.

Soelle has a metaphoric gift for evoking such indifference: 'Death is a life that is nothing but surviving. Because we live for bread alone, we die by bread alone' (*IR*, 6). Discerning a dehumanisation of spiritual sensibility in the rich world, she captures it through an image of a supermarket without relationship: 'absent-mindedly, yet at the same time absorbed in what we are doing, we push our shopping carts up one aisle and down the other while death and alienation have the run of the place' (*IR*, 8). For her, the crisis of faith in the West is not just a question of people who deny the existence of God or the relevance of religion; a deeper lack of faith goes hand in hand with a lack of real hope or love. Something essential to our full humanity is crushed, more by how we live than by how we think. Quietly but effectively, the system of the market is able to stifle any creative resistance.

Soelle came to understand that for two reasons contemplative and imaginative expressions of faith were particularly needed today: to liberate ourselves from consumerist superficiality and to convey the mystery of God's presence in suffering. On this second theme she frequently quotes Meister Eckhart: 'God is always with us in suffering' (*S*, 97). She refuses to indulge in old-style theodicy, defending God's role in the pain of the world, and doing so in a rationalist manner. Especially following her visits to Latin America, Soelle's approach to faith became more courageously narrative and imaginative. In her view, we have to listen reverently to the stories of victims in order to fuel a passion for justice in the spirit of Christ. As a result of her own solidarity with victims, she found herself stressing the link between the mystical and the poetic as a wavelength more worthy of God and of the realities of the poor. 'What really happens in mystical union is not a new vision of God but a different relationship to the world – one that has borrowed the eyes of God' (*SC*, 293). Faced with the question of God and the scandal of suffering, she found inspiration in a phrase of Eckhart: 'without a why' (*sunder warumbe*): faith needed to reject a merely intellectual or pragmatic wavelength in order to discover one more in tune with the mysteries of suffering and of love.

It is fascinating to see how Soelle moves towards a more experimental method in theology, open to different expressions of faith, including her own writing of poetry. She also became less reticent about autobiographical honesty. She tells of one television interview in which she commented on the costly nature of faith: 'one can believe only after one is dead' (*IR*, 29). When asked if this was her own personal experience, she found herself admitting, to her surprise, that it was connected with the pain of her divorce. This moment of unplanned self-revelation led her to realise that the fragility of faith needs a non-discursive language and more eloquent embodiments of religious experience. Instead of academic expressions of theology, she proposed a kind of 'theopoetry'. 'What do prayer and poetry in common? They connect us with our hopes' (*DSEW*, 177) Faith, in short, needs the courage to speak imaginatively, subjectively, and honestly – admitting the darkness and the doubt inherent in religious commitment. Thus in one of her later texts she wrote: 'For me, praying and writing poetry, prayer and poem, are not alternatives. The message I wish to pass on is meant to encourage people to learn to speak for themselves' (*DSEW*, 231).

Some theologians could object that Soelle's 'radical immanence' goes too far. God is indeed our capacity for love but more than that. The Resurrection is existential but more than that. A reaction against doctrine and against institutional religion can tempt her into too humanistic a version of faith. But perhaps these potential difficulties are a product of her desire to give faith a new cultural and social energy for today. Her overall vision of faith is rich in its convergence of different elements: the battle to rescue the Christian image of God from mere theism; her passionate and life-long dedication to a socially committed faith; her quest to forge a more literary language for theology and spirituality; her insistence on the connection between liberation and mysticism. In this way she challenges any reflection on faith to 'enlarge its tent' (as Isaiah said) by grounding itself in the struggles of history and by going beyond a faith that can seem to make no earthly difference.

An extended counter-cultural family

This more activist understanding of faith offered by Soelle is shared by many other more recent theologians. There is a whole family of thinkers who insist on the relevance of social contexts and the need for faith to be counter-cultural. Starting from this critical perspective, they explore such themes as memory, narrative, praxis and liberation. Therefore instead of an imaginary monologue, as in previous chapters, here I will seek to offer a quick anthology of Soelle's 'cousins', so to speak. In different ways, they all share an urgency about how the praxis of faith should respond to dehumanising forces in the culture.

These include figures as diverse as Johann Baptist Metz, Michael Warren, René Girard, Stanley Hauerwas, John F. Kavanaugh and Gustavo Gutiérrez. Indeed Pope Benedict XVI's 2009 encyclical, *Caritas in Veritate*, acknowledges the presence of sin in the structures of society and proposes 'relationality' as an essential human characteristic over against 'a search for individual well-being, limited to the gratification of psychological desires' (*Caritatis in Veritate* § 55). There is a conflict in our self-images between the individualist model inherited from the

Enlightenment and the model of inter-relationship which that encyclical links to God as Trinity.

Girard offers a provocative reading of culture as conflictual. He sees the history of humanity from the beginning as marked by perpetual violence. Why? Because our desires and imaginations are contaminated by 'rivalry', that is, a tendency to see others as invaders of our space and enemies to our freedom. This amounts to a universally inherited addiction, and, in Girard's view, religion, when it is lived genuinely, offers our only path of liberation from this illness. Rather like Soelle, he sees Christ as uniquely free of this contagion of hostility. The Cross embodies a radical love where we can learn to unlearn our distorted imagining and violence. That unlearning is at the heart of the long journey of faith, and hence faith is inevitably counter-cultural.

'Who is imagining your life for you' is a challenging question that Michael Warren has proposed for youth ministry. There are at least two important implications here: that an important battle-ground of our culture lies in imagination rather than in ideas, and that in this area of our 'social imaginary' (Taylor) we can be less free than we think. Cultural forces invade our imagination to sell us what Soelle called trivial images of ourselves. Warren also insists that Christian faith needs to embody that its difference of vision in concrete community practices.

Hauerwas, much influenced by Karl Barth, goes further in insisting on a necessary tension between faith and culture, and he too locates the war zone in human imagination. In words that are reminiscent of Soelle he claims that 'our society is a vast supermarket of desire in which each of us in encouraged to stand alone'. When the tyranny of individualism reigns, faith can be reduced to individual therapy, offering private comfort that ignores the suffering of the world. Whereas the surrounding culture lives as if God were dead, faith needs to be made concrete in a shared life-styles rather than in more spiritual interpretations. It is rooted in an alternative narrative of God's action, very different from the escapist narratives of the culture. 'The Christian imagination forces us to acknowledge that the world is different from what it seems' and therefore 'imagination formed by the stories and practices of the Church constitutes the ultimate realism'. Hauerwas argues provocatively that faith without enemies is incomprehensible and if faith does not see the call to be counter-cultural, it underestimates both the scandal of the Gospel and the corruption of the culture.

John Kavanaugh is a philosopher who keeps a watchful eye on North American culture and on its global influence, and has become an eloquent advocate of a spirituality of Christian critique and resistance. In particular he diagnoses a battlefield of images where two 'competing life-forms' confront one another: an emphasis on the person or else on commodities. There is a battle over what is truly 'real' – things or relationships, and faith reveals to us a particular understanding of relationships. It warns us of our perennial temptation to create and worship idols, or indeed to live too innocently within an 'idolatrous belief system'. Do we exist for 'narcissistic buying' and mechanistic efficiency, or else to learn the pilgrim road of self-sacrificing love? These are fundamental choices concerning how we see ourselves as persons. 'The acceptance or rejection of our vulnerability' is in fact a gateway to faith or a locked door against the possibility of another kind of love. Even religion itself can become enslaved unknowingly to the deceptive values of the culture, and hence the constant need of the prophetic tradition of self-critique.

The work of Johann Baptist Metz also resonates with many of Soelle's concerns, including a constant reality-check against the horrors of Auschwitz. He too sought to enlarge the focus from the existential quest of the individual to a more 'political theology', recognising that faith is influenced, for better or worse, by the assumptions of its social context. Therefore he criticised the tendency to privatise faith, making it mainly a personal relationship with God. In this spirit he came to distance himself from his mentor Karl Rahner, sensing that the Rahnerian approach lacked a social dimension. Instead of seeing the question of faith mainly as a problem of knowledge, Metz saw it as a practical issue involving the commitments we live out in today's context. He stressed the need for 'socially contextualized praxis' and of the Church as a space of critical freedom. Like Soelle, he underlined the crucial role of memory and of narrative in nourishing faith, adding that 'dangerous memory' is what we receive from revelation, the Gospels themselves being subversive of our cultural complacencies. Faith, therefore, is proved, not by intellectual argument, but by the praxis it provokes in the community of believers.

Even a short list of companion spirits for Soelle cannot omit Gustavo Gutiérrez, the Peruvian priest (and now a Dominican) whose book *A Theology of Liberation* (1971) is often credited with starting the movement of liberation theology and who has also written much on the link between theology and spirituality. His constant refrain is an invitation to see the world from the perspective of the poor, and in this way to enlarge how one interprets and lives the Christian faith. Whereas European theology was preoccupied with secularisation and non-belief, Gutiérrez claimed that in Latin America the main problem was that of the non-person, the oppressed and marginalised. Reading the Gospel in solidarity with the poor changes one's religious priorities. Faith is no longer identified with belief but with committed love. Recently Gutiérrez has quoted Pope Benedict's encyclical *Deus caritas est* as saying that 'love of God and love of neighbour have become one', adding that this intuition, when seen from the world of the poor, can become the foundation for a liberation spirituality, one that refuses to be disconnected from the inhuman social reality of so many people. In words reminiscent of Soelle, he comments that 'contemplation and solidarity are two sides of a practice'. Hence the 'preferential option for the poor' is an application of the core biblical vision as expressed in the Beatitudes or in the parable of the last judgement (in Matthew 25). If a spirituality of faith today neglects the unjust suffering all around us, it betrays the God of whom it speaks.

These various commentators all tend to stress the gulf between faith and culture and to portray faith as constantly embattled within enemy territory. There is an urgent and important truth in this, but there are also questions to be raised about the tone of our being counter-cultural. Is there at danger of a subtle fundamentalism here, tending to make blanket judgements and to forget that the Spirit is at work in all cultures? Or is there a temptation to scapegoat the culture for all the difficulties encountered by faith today? Whatever such reservations, the faith map offered by Soelle and her companions indicates an uphill and demanding route. With prophetic vehemence they will not let us forget the cry of our social contexts, and the deadness, as Scripture says, of any faith without works.

References to works of Dorothee Soelle

CL   *Choosing Life*, London, 1981.
IR   *The Inward Road and the Way Back*, London, 1975.
S   *Suffering*, London, 1975.
SG   *The Silent Cry: Mysticism and Resistance*, Minneapolis, 2001.
TG   *Thinking about God*, Philadelphia, 1990.
TS   *Theology for Sceptics*, London, 1995.
DSEW *Dorothee Soelle: Essential Writings*, ed. Dianne Oliver, New York, 2006.

8

Charles Taylor: the pressures of modernity

In 1960, when Charles Taylor was a graduate student in Oxford, he published an article entitled 'Clericalism', critical of the marginal role given to lay people in the Catholic Church. This showed, he argued, a defensive Church, isolated from modern culture, and slow to appreciate the new humanism that had come to birth over recent centuries. Such a ghetto stance was unfaithful to the Incarnation, because Christian faith invites us to move towards God through our humanity and through the changing adventure of history.

This youthful article came two years before the opening the Second Vatican Council. In subsequent decades, as the work of this Canadian philosopher became widely known, his books often touched on religious themes without ever making them central. However his Catholicism has become a more explicit presence in his writings in the last ten years or so (beginning with *A Catholic Modernity* of 1999). In 2008, for instance, he wrote a short reflection on the barriers between the university world and religion. His critique is now directed against a different form of academic clericalism, whereby philosophers, sociologists and historians find it normal to ignore the spiritual dimension of life. Such intellectuals, he holds, have not only forgotten the answers to the great questions of life, they have forgotten the questions.

Beyond human flourishing

Although Taylor is a moral and political philosopher rather than a specifically religious thinker, he offers us a perspective not found in more theological authors. In particular, his explorations of cultural history can help us to understand the effect of changing contexts on faith. Context conditions consciousness, as a Marxist emphasis would have it, and the 'modern' consciousness of the individual has been a constant theme in Taylor's work. He has explored in depth the influence of this emerging self-image on our religious horizons

– or lack of them. Especially in recent writings, he has tried to understand our spiritual situation as living in an age dominated by secularity, and he invites us to stop moaning about statistical or sociological loss of faith and to ask deeper questions.

Comments on the nature and importance of faith occur with increasing frequency in Taylor's work, often stressing that religious belief is richer than the usual cultural perception of it. For instance, he rejects the assumption 'that the main point of religion is solving the human need for meaning' (*SA*, 718), because he suspects this approach of being influenced by a pervasive individualism that measures everything in terms of self-fulfilment. Instead, he presents religion as a source of graced conversion, where 'the perspective of a transformation of human beings' takes them beyond what 'is normally understood as human flourishing' (*SA*, 430). As Taylor has remarked, a purely social or functional account of religion would be like Hamlet without the Prince.

What he sees as specific to Christian faith is captured in this sentence: 'God's initiative is to enter, in full vulnerability, the heart of the resistance, to be among humans, offering participation in the divine life' (*SA*, 654). Against more agnostic or psychological viewpoints, he stresses that Christian revelation empowers people through their sharing in God's own love. In an eloquent passage in *A Catholic Modernity*, he wonders how such a high vision of love can become real today and he writes: 'our being in the image of God is also our standing among others in the stream of love [which ultimately is] the Trinity. Now it makes a whole lot of difference whether you think this kind of love is a possibility for us humans. I think it is, but only to the extent that we open ourselves to God' (*CM*, 35). This seems a remarkable statement of faith commitment, all the more impressive since it comes from a world-famous philosopher.

From his perspective as a specialist in cultural history Taylor underlines that faith 'has survived … by evolving' (*VRT*, 104). Moreover, he is convinced that God is gradually 'educating mankind' by 'transforming it from within' (*SA*, 668). Even a time of cultural upheaval can purify images of God which were 'too simple, too anthropocentric, too indulgent' (*VRT*, 57). He also suggests that 'we are just at the beginning of a new age of religious searching, whose outcome no one can foresee' (*SA*, 535), but when faith will be less 'collective [and] more christocentric' (*SA*, 541). It will also need 'a new poetic language' (*SA*, 757). In this he echoes the emphasis on imagination that we have seen in theological writers as different as Newman, Balthasar and Soelle. For Taylor the hope is to nourish faith today through moments of 'epiphany', akin to the experience of art as a call from beyond the self, because in this way we discover 'moral sources *outside* the subject which resonate *within*' (*SS*, 510).

The complex story of modernity

The first chapter of his enormous book, *A Secular Age*, published in 2007, begins with a question: 'why was it virtually impossible not to believe in God in, say, 1500 in our Western society, while in 2000 many of us find this not only easy, but even inescapable?' His answer involves the birth of a 'modern' sense of the self, as less embedded in traditions of belonging, more insistent on individual rights, and assuming that this 'disengaged' version of self is simply common sense. But 'human nature is something that ... cannot be conceived as existing in a single individual' (*CM*, 113). In this spirit Taylor defends the importance of community roots and 'mutual enrichment' as opposed to 'solitary self-sufficiency' (*CM*, 114, 116). He is sympathetic to the 'modern' ideal of personal authenticity and yet suspicious of its more dehumanising embodiments, in particular of its tendency to get out of touch with sources of meaning larger than the individual self. Among these larger horizons is the possibility of religious faith.

Taylor is frequently impatient with approaches to secular modernity that provide only surface descriptions of what he considers a more complex story. What he calls 'acultural' theories of modernity are merely sociological in the sense of explaining secularisation as the automatic product of urbanisation, or the inevitable outcome of scientific rationality. According to this interpretation modernity would be like an automatic steamroller, levelling out traditions, local cultures and religious faith. The mistake of this 'acultural' school is to see everything through the lens of Western history and to interpret decline of religion only in terms of loss of beliefs, thinking that science and the new individualism make the truth claims of Christianity incredible.

Instead Taylor seeks to deepen the agenda of discussion from the world of ideas to the more hidden world of self-images. Again and again he insists that the loss of faith associated with Western modernity is less a crisis of truth or epistemology than of ethics and of imagination. He holds that secularisation has to do with our moral self-understanding, and more particularly with our 'social imaginary'. This expression refers to our ways of imaging our lives – before theory comes along to analyse or explain things. It points to 'that largely unstructured and inarticulate understanding of our whole situation' (*MSI*, 25) which serves as a background music of our lived assumptions.

In ways reminiscent of Newman (whom, surprisingly, he never mentions) Taylor defends this less intellectual or pre-logical approach to meaning: ordinary people give meaning to their lives not through explicit ideas but through narratives, images, and shared practices in community. Whereas the 'acultural' model neglects this area of moral sensibility, a 'cultural' interpretation locates the crisis of faith in changes of symbolic imagination. It is more than simply the by-product of external social factors or new theories of knowledge. Indeed, it would be a form of Western arrogance to claim that one particular pattern of secularisation must be repeated in other cultures whenever they become technologically 'modern'.

Time, ordinary life, inwardness

Taylor, in brief, interprets the drama of modernity as a revolution of cultural sensibility, and not simply as a sociologically predictable set of external changes. He goes on to insist that although certain forms of faith have gone into crisis, the core of Christian faith transcends its changing cultural embodiments. Thus he seeks to lead debates on secularisation into more tacit and subjective fields, seeing modernity as more than a product of the usual suspects – the rationalism born between Descartes and the Enlightenment, or the political or sociological upheavals, ranging from revolution to urbanisation. Among the factors that he sees as creating a radically different culture are the market economy, the development of a public sphere of print media, and the birth of popular democracy based on the sovereignty of the people. But he is more interested (and interesting) about the impact of these situations on what he calls the social imaginary, in other words how people come to feel and interpret their lives at an intuitive level. He complains that too often we speak of 'modernity as a traditional society minus something', seeing it as either liberation from or as loss of older religious horizons (*CM*, 107). Instead he holds that 'the modern theory of moral order' could never have become dominant 'in our culture without this penetration/transformation of our imaginary' (*SA*, 175).

Underlying this transformation, he sees a different human perception of time, whereby time loses its vertical dimension of life as related to the eternal or transcendent, and becomes largely horizontal. This sense of non-religious time allows people, for the first time in history, to 'imagine society horizontally unrelated to any "high points"' (*MSI*, 157), so that they come to understand and imagine themselves 'exclusively in secular time' (*SA*, 714). A second development has to do with 'the affirmation of ordinary life' (*SA*, 370) as morally valuable in itself. This is connected with the Protestant emphasis on work and the family life, and with its generally non-sacramental theology. A third development is the centrality of the individual and of 'new forms of inwardness' (*CM*, 107). Unfortunately, this initially positive emphasis on subjectivity will later descend into the ambiguous 'ethic of self-fulfilment in relationships' (*MSI*, 103) and, in more recent times this separated self has become more marked by therapeutic self-expression, consumerism and a tendency to see sin only as sickness. Taylor does not mince his words: this shrinking of subjectivity can 'actually end up abasing' human dignity (*SA*, 618).

A new sense of God

Connected with his concerns for these dimensions – time, ordinary existence, subjectivity – is Taylor's typical focus on human identity. Modernity spells the end of an older world of stable religious identity, marked by 'social embeddedness' and a hierarchical world view. It involves a new moment of history where individuals are seen as responsible for imagining and choosing their own sense of self. 'Secularity' enters the scene when the motivation for action feels no need to look beyond the here and now in order to find foundations for its commitment.

Taylor is never a naïve celebrant of this modernity. He admits that it 'is often read through its least impressive, most trivializing aspects' (*SS*, 511). Many of its achievements, in his view, have a shadow side, where they slide into shrunken versions of an original ideal. There has been a struggle between higher and lower forms of freedom. The new rationality can become merely functional or utilitarian. A closed individualism can forget larger questions of meaning, or reduce freedom to egoist horizons, where 'more self-centred modes of self-fulfilment betray the ideal of authenticity' (*EA*, 105). In more recent decades this betrayal has shown itself in the 'soft relativism' of each person doing 'their own thing' (*SA*, 484). Such reductive versions of the hopes of modernity happen when-ever we forget both our responsibility for others and our innate desire for some connection with God.

With this background he evaluates the impact of cultural change on religious faith. Over the years he has constantly repeated that secular modernity does not necessarily mean 'the absence of reli-gion' but rather that 'religion occupies a different place' in people's experience and imagination (*MSI*, 194). More specifically, moder-nity 'removed one mode in which God was formerly present', perceived as reigning in a vertical and transcendent eternity, but an 'alternative form of God's presence' becomes possible, more per-sonal or spiritual, less institutional, less exclusively transcendent or eschatological (*MSI*, 186–7). In Taylor's words, 'in personal life the dissolution of the enchanted world can be compensated by … a strong sense of the involvement of God in my life' (*MSI*, 193). Thus a different language of faith comes to birth which involves all of our humanity and is much more than an intellectual belief.

Accompanying this attempt to identify new cultural expressions of faith, he questions whether we should give priority to the individual or to the community. He worries about the excessive isolation of the separated individual produced by modernity. He sees a need to retrieve relationships and responsibilities as central to an authentically human self-image. But the widespread assumption is that society is made up of individuals: 'are we not by nature and essence individuals?' If this idea dominates, it can lead us to abandon 'modes of complementarity' and mutual belonging that have characterised most of human history (*MSI*, 18). Taylor comes out in favour of a relational or communal anthropology as a necessary foundation for human selfhood. Isolated forms of identity remain fragile or even self-deceptive: 'to be an individual is not to be a Robinson Crusoe, but to be placed in a certain way among other humans' (*MSI*, 65).

Spirituality today

Taylor's most extended reflection on his own Catholicism and on Christian themes in general can be found in his 1999 lecture at the University of Dayton, 'A Catholic Modernity'. Here he sets himself the task of imitating Matteo Ricci, the Jesuit missionary who entered sympathetically into the culture of China in the late sixteenth century. In similar fashion Taylor prefers to stress common ground rather than adopting a strongly counter-cultural stance. He distances himself from the closed or 'exclusive humanism' inherited from modernity, which in his view tends to forget the human need for a deeper or higher wholeness of life. But he is equally uneasy with 'the project of Christendom', or any model where faith seeks to rule the culture or to achieve some fusion between religion and society.

Christians should thank Voltaire and his like for the humbling but liberating experience of dismantling Christendom, thus 'allowing us to live the Gospel in a purer way' (*CM*, 18). They should also acknowledge that certain Gospel-based values, for instance, human rights, have flourished more effectively in a secular setting. However, Taylor qualifies this by insisting that 'the denial of transcendence can put the most valuable gains of modernity in danger' (*CM*, 30). Without a sense of God, can the human values born from the Judeo-Christian tradition survive for long? Can the primacy of ordinary life avoid becoming a shrunken zone of self-concern? As against isolated or disengaged individualism, he suggests a more relational perspective: 'to see the fullness of life as something that happens between people rather than within each one' (*CM*, 113). Identity at its best comes from recognition in relationship, not simply from a solo run through life. Indeed, without a framework or tradition of belonging there is a danger of falling 'into a life that is spiritually senseless'(*SS*, 18).

Taylor has no doubt that modernity helped believers to emerge from more puritan, more fearful and excessively other-worldly versions of faith, and to recognise 'the potential of human beings for goodness' (*CM*, 32). Indeed a transition from a more ascetical spirituality to one that reads the Gospel as promising fullness in this life has become one of the hallmarks of today's religious culture. Here too, however, a danger lurks: can this sensibility face the darker sides of life? Taylor sees secular humanism as too innocent on this point, and he implies that some versions of spirituality fall into a 'feel-good' naivety. Genuine fullness of life 'means eternal life and death is taken in stride' (*CM* 110). In this lecture, as so often in his work, Taylor's original contribution lies in his changing the agenda of the debate about modernity, religion and culture. As already indicated, what he calls the 'main story' is best understood as a shift of sensibility rather than of ideas: 'the obstacles to belief in Western modernity are primarily moral and spiritual', not simply a question of truth or intellectual credibility (*CM*, 25). It is on this level of non-explicit, but lived, assumptions that he is concerned about long-term damage to humanity, when it tries to live without any religious dimension to life.

A different love

That 1999 lecture ends with a reflection on cultural discernment in the light of a 'stream of love' descending from God as Trinity, where Taylor urges us to be healthily 'bewildered' by the complexity of living the Christian faith today. We should not fall into the extremes of embracing everything or condemning everything – what he calls the 'boosters' or 'knockers' of our culture. 'As with Ricci, the Gospel message to this time and society has to respond both to what in it already reflects the life of God and to the doors which have been closed against this life' (*CM*, 37). Responding to a debate on his lecture, Taylor goes further in expressing his religious positions. He speaks of the pain of students who are religious believers but who find themselves in universities that silence their spiritual dimension or impose a kind of atheist conformity. 'Unbelief has informed more than the answers; it has also shaped the questions' (*CM*, 119). In his own field of moral philosophy, he fears that there is room only for neutral theory about what we should do, but no place for reflecting on how to motivate goodness in practice. Neither is there any recognition of a perennial conflict between our 'loving and self-absorbed desires' (*CM*, 121). When 'there is a lot of hostility out there', Christian academics should try 'to change the agenda, open it up', unlocking 'the closed and neglected corridors in the ethical mansion' (*CM*, 123). He sees the present level of anger in cultural debates as blocking 'spiritual growth' and even 'resisting God', and he ends with a challenging insight on communicating faith today: 'changing the tone might be the essential prelude to changing the content' (*CM*, 124–5).

Towards transformative faith

In the several years before publishing *A Secular Age* in 2007, Taylor began to tackle religious themes more often and more openly, not necessarily through reading theology but through reflecting on writers such as Hopkins, Flannery O'Connor or Bede Griffiths. The final chapter of that volume voices a critique of a trivial level of cultural unbelief and also of ecclesial paralysis in meeting the spiritual needs of people today. It offers a prophetic summary of his hopes for the survival of faith. Inspired by his reading of Ivan Illich, Taylor writes passionately about the need for more incarnational expressions of faith. Under the subtle erosion of the dominant culture, faith can lose its transformative edge. Models of thought, even in theology, can be cramped by the assumption that objectivity requires us to see truth 'as something quite independent of us'. He views this as a dangerous 'excarnation' of reason, a forgetting of commitment and affectivity as valid roads to knowledge (*SA*, 746).

Unless Christians have the courage to 'recover a sense what the Incarnation can mean' (*SA*, 753), even the power of the Eucharist can be strangled by convention. Taylor maintains that authentic faith has to do with our gradual conversion by God's love and towards a new way of loving with God. Clearly this perspective goes beyond any tendency to examine religion sociologically. Here the surprise of the Gospel has to do with God's transformative action in our lives: if we over-identify faith with the values of the culture, we will miss this 'greater transformation which Christian faith holds out' (*SA*, 737) – that we participate in God and that this is the source of our difference. Such a specifically faith-based image rescues us from the loneliness of modernity where 'all meaning comes from us' and where 'we encounter no echo beyond' the world of immanence (*SA*, 376).

That a major contemporary philosopher could arrive at such affirmations about faith is remarkable. It shows that we cannot do justice to the fullness of faith either by fidelity to the dominant rationality or by innocently embracing the ideals of the culture. According to Taylor, our sources of goodness and of loving need to be larger than the self. Even though he admires and defends the emergence of the modern sense of self, he has become troubled about the unanchored and 'buffered' personality – isolated from others, from traditions of meaning, ultimately from the possibility of religious faith as the most credible fountain of our transformation towards love. When that horizon becomes real, life becomes an adventure of 'choosing ourselves in the light of the infinite' (*SS*, 449).

In the voice of Taylor (*an imaginary monologue*)

We need to take on board the hugeness of the cultural revolution we have experienced, and continue to experience. It involves more than some easily explainable social changes, and more than a different set of ideas. In place of a previously stable identity, people now find themselves in an ocean of cross currents, of multiple identities on the move. This new context also means a painful and sudden uprooting of religious self-images. It has displaced Church-based religion from its previous centrality: forms of religious belonging and expression that once seemed so secure have come to appear unreal, out of touch or even oppressive.

A deeper secularisation

Religious belief used to be the default option for most people, but unbelief or at least a large-scale unchurching has taken its place. The cultural situation has swung from a smooth pre-modern inheritance of meaning to a fast 'disembedding' along 'modern' lines, as an ambiguous individualism became dominant. In today's so-called post-modern world, everyone tells us that we suffer, as never before, from fragmentation, dispersal, or drifting. And so the agenda of faith, and the whole context of our receiving and deciding, has changed radically.

For years I have insisted that the real process of secularisation is not found in sociological statistics of religious diminishment, and that a deeper erosion occurs in our unformulated but shared images of spiritual identity. Is our visible and horizontal life everything, or are there higher and vertical calls, inviting us beyond what we glimpse with our empirical eyes? Certainly the dominant culture around pressurises us to forget our higher hungers and to lost ourselves in the glamorous surfaces of life.

Faced with such enormous change, it is vital to remember that our freedom to respond creatively is never extinguished. Don't expect me to give directives about faith formation. I'm just a philosopher with a passion for exploring the deeper shifts of history, of our self-interpretations and how we live them. But I am also a Catholic, increasingly inclined to ponder the emerging languages of faith today and indeed the whole issue of the future of Christianity – all in the light of some converging insights I have accumulated over the years.

Beyond neutrality

Modernity has taught us to value neutrality, or a certain kind of objectivity, and this can leave us handicapped concerning paths of existential commitment. We all live from various options, but we fear that they cannot be justified rationally. Here we are suffering from an idolatry of clarity, or of clarity of a certain Cartesian kind. But our human knowing is so much richer than what we can articulate with intellectual precision.

Religious faith is a genuine kind of knowledge, but not one that fits into the straitjacket of our inherited empiricism or rationalism.

As part of the history of the self, I have been a constant defender of the positive achievements of modernity, such as its ideal of personal authenticity. But we should not deny the later tendency to reduce the personal to the merely individual, or to shrink authenticity into self-fulfilment without conscience. We need to critique these cultural forms of a drifting existence as more likely to undermine the possibility of Christian faith than any of the intellectual attacks of angry atheists.

My hunch is that religious formation today needs to be doubly discerning. It needs to be critical of the dehumanising factors in the culture that rob people of spiritual awareness. This is not a matter of scapegoating the dominant life-styles but of asking questions about the deadening impact they can have on our self-horizons. And then there is a call for Christians to be honestly self-critical of their own structures and their own reductions of the grit of the Gospel. Christian history is marked by terrible scandals that can make one despair of our Church and of ourselves. My own hesitant hope is that after facing the shadows of history in a spirit of mourning, we can become more creative in shaping our always inadequate embodiments of faith.

A key dimension of humanity

I sometimes speak of my religious 'hunches', and perhaps that word is deliberately tentative, because a philosopher is not meant to wear his faith on his sleeve in university circles. In old age I have been rebelling more frequently against that silent academic censorship. What are some of these hunches that have strengthened for me into strong convictions? That religion is a crucial and universal dimension of our humanity, and that to ignore this possibility is to risk not just spiritual but anthropological impoverishment.

I have come to see that a neutral approach to religion is reductive. If Christianity is true, it offers more than an answer to my hunger for anchors in a confusing world: it is rooted in an extraordinary event of God in history and one that continues to happen in us. It involves an almost incredible sharing in God's love rather than just institutional belonging or believing. Christ is our source of transformation now, rather than merely a founder of a tradition in the past. The historical and functional interpretations of religion are valid approaches, but they should not monopolise our vision. To echo the Gospel, there is something more than Solomon here.

For years, experts in theology and religious education have been saying that faith has to be a decision, not just a passive transmission (a terrible word more suited to car engines). That stress on choice is valid but it is not enough. The decision is not just about a religious truth but about a whole way of life, a different vision of everything, ultimately about receiving and responding to a divine love called *agape*. Don't ask me for help about how to communicate this to a new generation. My hunch, to repeat that word, is that it is always easier to 'teach religion' functionally and historically, and no doubt that is needed. But more importantly, any spiritual conversion needs to be prepared and pointed towards, if people are to arrive at a liveable faith for today and tomorrow. I have come to think of poets as our best spiritual guides, because they can tap into our imagination and put us in contact with possibilities that get suppressed in routine thinking or living.

Fullness as gift

For years I have been fascinated by our longing for fullness and for human flourishing in its many forms. Although I recognise, with deep respect, the genuineness of non-religious versions of fullness and flourishing, I am convinced that the religious road is more true and more in tune with our hopes. In the Christian vision fullness and flourishing come as gifts in a relationship, not simply as self-achievements. I hold that the origin of all our growing in love has to be larger than us. I worry that unanchored individuals – isolated or uprooted from

adition – are being deprived of religious faith as the most
ible source of transformation towards that larger love.

f I were ever to write more explicitly about Christian
spirituality, perhaps the epigraph of the book could come from
the prologue of John's Gospel: 'from Christ's fullness we have
all received'. In this light I would want to evoke not only the
joys but also the fragilities of faith, its darknesses and dangers,
and the long adventure of trying to make the Gospel incarnate
again within all the changes of history.

References to works of Charles Taylor

CM   *A Catholic Modernity*, ed. J. Heft, Oxford, 1999.

EA   *The Ethics of Authenticity*, Cambridge MA, 1991.

MSI *Modern Social Imaginaries*, Durham NC, 2004.

SA   *A Secular Age*, Cambridge MA, 2007.

SS   *Sources of the Self: The Making of Modern Identity*, Cambridge MA, 1989.

VRT *Varieties of Religion Today*, Cambridge MA, 2002.

9

Pierangelo Sequeri: horizons of trust

Our youngest faith explorer deserves to be better known in the English-speaking world, but so far none of his many books has been translated from Italian. He is a leading member of the Milan Faculty of Theology, and is also well known as a composer and as creator of a school of music therapy for mentally disabled people. Like many other thinkers explored in previous chapters here, Sequeri is keen to get beyond a cold rationality in theology and to develop a richer language for faith reflection. Since the Reformation, we Catholics have tended to stress religious belief as an intellectual assent, so much so that we often forget other dimensions of faith that had recognised and appreciated in previous ages. We have said that faith involves a free decision, but we have seldom asked how we actually live that freedom. We have not denied that faith can involve a person's feelings, but we have relegated affectivity to what was (vaguely) called spirituality. As long as the old cognitive model dominated, faith was thought of as a question of accepting truths about God. In spite of the great tradition of Christian art, many images in our Churches were devoid of depth, as if we had forgotten that faith has something to do with beauty. Sequeri's theology sets out to heal these various forms of forgetfulness and impoverishment. Truth, in his view, needs to rediscover its relationship with at least three neglected zones – freedom, affectivity and beauty. We cannot, he holds, recognise religious truth without making a option for love, without our hearts being touched, and without being in some way overwhelmed by the beauty and the strangeness of God.

Discerning the damage

Perhaps the best entrance into Sequeri's thinking on faith is through his critique of dangers that he discerns in today's culture. First of all, he distrusts the version of reasoning born of scientific modernity and highlights the damage it did to theology. A narrow rationality produced a shrunken image of who we are and of how we should approach truth. When theology tried to imitate this scientific method, it neglected the drama of religious experience and the lived encounter with revelation. It made an idol of clear doctrines (essential in themselves) and therefore separated religious truth from our everyday adventure of learning to love. This whole approach to faith also gave the impression of a despotic God or else of a deist 'Explanation of the Universe' (note the echoes of Soelle). In this way, theology became strangely silent on the realities of Christian believing, including what Ruth Burrows has described as the light-on/light-off pendulum of personal faith.

A second problem arises from the inheritance of modernity. If its dominant image of truth was too impersonal, the modern model of freedom was that of the self-sufficient individual, someone who had no need for religious faith or the transformation it might entail. Sequeri is deeply suspicious of this kind of self-fulfilment, comparing it to the legendary King Midas: everything it touches turns into self-destructive narcissism. Modernity, in short, 'froze the divine', 'eroded the subject', and did not envisage a 'trustable truth'.

If the new picture of rationality and of freedom tended to exclude the possibility of faith, a third battleground went largely unnoticed. Theology was so concerned with answering the rational challenge of the Enlightenment that it overlooked a major cultural revolution of the same period. Sequeri thinks of the Romantic movement as an authentic but ambiguous attempt to defend our spiritual potentials. It started with artists and poets who resisted the grey world of the industrial revolution and a merely empirical approach to truth. Romantic sensibility appealed to people's feelings and continues to have a far-reaching influence in today's post-modern world. Rather like Charles Taylor, Sequeri points to a risk that the romantic emphasis on personal feeling can easily shrink into lonely individualism. He also sees us as suffering from divided consciousness: our capacity to cope wisely with change has not kept pace with the technical complexity of our lives; and our typical modes of thinking remain cut off from our deeper needs. In 2001 he summed up his perspective in these words: 'The question of the spiritual dignity of the human – and of the Christian quality of faith – seem to me an enormous challenge facing western culture' (*SS*, ix). In his view, the world of faith needs a renewed kind of reasoning, and the world of reason needs to re-connect with the spiritual depths of our humanity.

Remembering a famous nursery rhyme, we could say that Sequeri sets out to put Humpty Dumpty together again – after a 'great fall'. If our models of truth have fallen into narrowness, and our images of freedom into closed self-realisation, how can we re-establish bridges between truth and freedom? The ordinary unfolding of existence involves so much that cannot be approached by the senses. In particular the truth of religious faith can never be verified through external evidence. (Sorry about that, Professor Dawkins.) When two people are so much in love that they decide to stay together for life, something more than neural or psychological compatibility has happened. Many layers of their humanity have come into play. Thus Sequeri asks us to widen the agenda of our thinking about faith, and in particular to allow for a convergence of at least five deep dimensions of ourselves – not only our sense of truth and of freedom, but also of ethics, of affectivity and of aesthetic perception. Otherwise Humpty Dumpty will remain in pieces, and we will fall short of a worthy level for exploring questions of faith.

To summarise the scene: culturally we have suffered from an unbalanced inheritance from modernity and in particular from three reductive forms of isolation. If what we call reason is identified with empirical verification, it may produce major triumphs in science, but causes a distortion in things human. If what we call freedom is identified with self-determination, a glorious gift of every human being shrinks into a small space. Again, if emotion becomes our exclusive guide, an important zone of humanity is exalted in ways that cut it off from its natural companions. If truth becomes separated from freedom and from feeling, we become handicapped in facing existential questions, because these personal fields need the whole self, involving our story, feelings, options, dispositions, and relationships. 'Our life of feelings is the great river in which we learn to appreciate what is truly decisive for us, what touches us and convinces, what asks for our commitment and calls forth our response' (*SVI*, 74).

Learning from aesthetics

Since he is a musician and composer, as well as a lecturer on art, it is hardly surprising that Sequeri agrees with those who advocate a retrieval of an aesthetic sense in theology. In 2000 he wrote: 'Without the mediation of imagination, our spirit can remain blind and speechless on the great questions of meaning. Our interiority does not really come alive without some symbolic mediation of the sensible' (*ED*, 13). At the heart of our experience of art, as he sees it, is a knowledge of the spiritual through our senses, but for too long theologians have tried to discuss faith without paying attention to feeling or beauty or experience. On the pretext of protecting some purity of truth, they have deprived us of seeing revelation as a gift that overwhelms and transforms us.

Yet our best encounter with art offers a fruitful analogy for faith because it calls us out of our little selves. Its impact is captured in a famous line at the end of a Rilke poem concerning the Miletus statue of Apollo in the Louvre, an ancient torso unearthed only in 1872 (also cited by Balthasar). The poet gazes at its fragmented grandeur, without head or arms or legs, only to find that it glows with primitive power and pronounces a kind of judgment. The poem ends:

> There is no spot of this stone,
> that does not see you. You must change your life.

Sequeri, in his different way, reminds us that the experience of faith includes something of that awakening to wonder, because it too involves a response to an overpowering presence. The difference is that now we are sought out by Divine Love become human in Christ. In this way the beauty of Christian revelation unites glory and tenderness. Like art, it involves a call from the Other to become other, but the encounter with Christ itself empowers us to change. In this light Sequeri insists that 'the connection between aesthetic experience and Christian spirituality needs to reclaim its right to citizenship in theology' (*ED*, 440).

Trust as gateway

To revisit the path of beauty is one way of saving us from false objectivity. Another avenue which receives attention in Sequeri's thinking is located in the interpersonal field. In ways that echo Newman (whom he never mentions), he insists that trust, which is fundamental for religious faith, is equally central in all human experience. So much of what we do relies on others. Without a disposition of trust, how could we live? Sequeri invites us to recognise how this universal dimension of our interpersonal experience takes us beyond any external yardstick and towards a more relational logic. But here he makes deeper claims than Newman did. Believing in others is part of our primordial anthropology. It is what makes us human. It is the source of our dignity. It is our most ordinary way of knowing. Have we become blind to this because we suffer from an over-identification of knowing with impersonal observation? Under the influence of this dominant assumption of our culture, we can lose trust in trust. We downgrade it to something secondary, and so it is seen as not really a central form of human knowing. But, argues Sequeri, we need to revisit the drama of our trusting in all its complexity and only then will we have a foundation for reflecting on the richness of religious faith. A main strand of his writings invites us to explore our ordinary capacity for trusting, seeing it as the key to our identity and indeed to our readiness for faith.

The act of trusting another person is by its nature relational, and therefore not lonely. It is rooted in a gradual recognition that the other person is worthy of our confidence. It is an act that unites thinking, deciding and feeling. In fact it is a universal characteristic shared by all humanity and where it is damaged or reduced, something tragic happens to people. It would be easy to misinterpret this emphasis as soft or sentimental, and hence in danger of divorcing faith from the need to think. Nothing could be further from Sequeri's intention. Rather, just as Ratzinger calls so often for an enlargement of reason, so Sequeri wants us to see faith as a fuller kind of knowing than any detached or neutral inquiry. An older theology made much ado about the 'credibility' of faith, and even that word can have narrowly intellectual overtones. It opted for a tone of cool or detached analysis. Instead Sequeri asks us to reflect on the trustworthiness of God, and that change of vocabulary indicates a different wavelength. As George Steiner claimed, in his classic *Real Presences*, there would be no history or art or religion without an initial act of trust. But for Sequeri the area of trust is also a battle zone. It is where we overcome our deep-seated temptation to suspicion and hostility, and where our constant swinging between trust and mistrust involves a battle between openness and closure to grace.

Among the various bridges to be re-built, one in particular is central for Sequeri: between our self-understanding (or anthropology) and our understanding of Christ (or Christology). Repeatedly he insists that our contemporary faith crisis stems from two sources – a reductive image of our own human potentials and a similarly reductive image of God – ultimately rooted in negativity or fear. He adds that the typical loss of faith today 'has to do with affectivity, not with ideas' because 'what has died is the feeling of a presence' of God in our lives (*IC*, 28). To counter the many forms of unbelief that stem from suspicion, he insists on our human capacity for trusting others as not only the core of our humanity but as our principal avenue of faith. In our ordinary experience, he argues, 'no revelation of another person can happen without establishing a relationship of trust' (*TD*, 143).

The prayer space of Christ

Once we understand the anthropological centrality of our human trusting, we can appreciate the disclosure of divine trust in Christ. Sequeri points us towards the pinnacle of trust that we can discover in the Abba relationship between Jesus and his Father. This is faith in its highest form. Here our human experience of trusting finds its crown and completion in the mutual trust between Father and Son. Here our religious imagination learns another level of trust by participating, so to speak, in the flow of God. Here we glimpse how all interpersonal knowing is crowned and inspired by the love between God the Father and His Son become man. 'Our life of feelings is the great river in which we learn to appreciate what is truly decisive for us, what touches us and convinces us, what asks for our commitment and calls forth our response' (*SVI*, 74). If this is so in human love, a similar but different expansion comes when we open ourselves to a faith-encounter with Christ and are invited into the unique space of his 'luminous relationship with Abba-God' (*IF*, 112).

Although Sequeri, as already seen, devotes much attention to cultural and spiritual dangers that can cramp our readiness for Christian revelation, the core of his positive theology of faith invites us to ponder the prayer of Christ himself. Although some theologians might have reservations about it, Sequeri is happy to talk of the faith of Christ in this sense. 'I see Jesus as electrified by an intuition or perception, one could even say by a faith in regard to God as Father' (*IC*, 55). In this sense he holds that we also discover our true identity through a contemplative approach to the faith of Jesus. The mystery of Christ's own identity is best discerned in this space of prayer-trust with the Father: in this unique relationship he was guided by a 'dazzling certainty about the absolute devotion of God towards humankind' (*IF*, 107). For Sequeri our road to fullness of Christian faith involves recognising the new vision born from Christ's Abba-Father experience: a sense of God as speaking to and fulfilling all our affectivity. Entering through grace into this space of Christ's prayer relationship, we come to realise who God is and also who we can be. Here all our longing for truth and justice come together on a new foundation.

Shock of Resurrection

If Sequeri gives unusual attention to this relational core of Christ's own spirituality, he also suggests another set of Gospel experiences as offering a key perspective on faith – the encounters of the disciples with the Risen Lord. Here it is always Jesus who takes the initiative to show himself, affectionately calling his friends towards a transforming recognition of newness. These moments represent for Sequeri 'the capacity of Jesus for making himself recognized with certainty in the Spirit as the living Son of the living God' (*DA*, 197). The faith that comes to birth here is not simply a matter of new insight but of insight accompanied by feelings of awe before an overwhelming novelty. And this experience of the disciples continues to be part of every journey of faith: they moved from 'unbelieving amazement' to the 'faith of witnesses', as they were led to reread their memories of the Galilee years (*DA*, 206). As the reality of Risen Love entered their imagination, they could gradually reinterpret everything with fresh eyes, and reach a totally different awareness of God's action in and through Jesus.

An older apologetics gave so much attention to external realism about the Resurrection that it downplayed this drama of recognition and its impact on the disciples. A recent book by the Australian theologian Anthony Kelly seems very much in agreement with Sequeri's emphasis. It argues that the impact of the Resurrection, as seen in the first disciples, inaugurates a distinctive wavelength of Christian rationality: 'The singularity of the resurrection event must in some way leave some forms of reason, and even theological reason, at a loss ... His rising from the dead stupefies all forms of logical reason' (*RE*, 7). Sequeri would also have us focus on faith as receptivity to the sheer excess of God. The encounter with the Risen Christ takes us beyond all normal rationality into a rationality of relational wonder, one that allows a convergence of many layers of our humanity – including understanding, emotion, freedom, gratitude – as they absorb an amazing novelty, the beauty and surprise of God's victory.

Gathering the strands

Even from these few pages, it will be obvious that Pierangelo Sequeri is an ambitious and difficult thinker. It is not easy to translate his ideas into a short space, and yet it has seemed worthwhile to try. Before finishing this part of the chapter, we can gather together some of the strands of his approach.

If our culture lives with shrunken self-images, it can easily disregard not just religious faith but all forms of faith. But what happens when we allow a work of art to reach our feelings or awaken our imagination, indicates a more personal path to meaning than the colder ways of rationality. So we need to find room for the aesthetic, the symbolic, the affective and the interpersonal, as deep avenues towards truth.

Belonging with others in mutual relationship is prior to any head knowledge. Our capacity for trust is born there and represents our most original form of human knowing. Affective trusting is the root of all our reasoning. From this cornerstone of our humanity we discover that religious faith continues and fulfils the more ordinary acts of faith that we live with other people.

We have faith before we have 'a faith'. When we recognise our fullest call in the Trust of Jesus, the anthropological becomes theological, and equally the theological becomes rooted in the drama of our history. In becoming theological, the anthropological discovers a fullness beyond all its imagining.

What privileged moments of friendship reveal – the beauty and power of our capacity for trust – is how we can approach the core relationship of Christ, as embodied in the Gospel accounts of his prayer. Here we glimpse the historical and yet eternal completion of our human hopes in Trinitarian mutual love. This reality of God-as-love is not reached as a verified fact but only as a trust encounter.

The activity of faith, on various levels, is central to who we are. It is a waking up to a relation, a possibility of trusting, a presence and a promise. It is a recognition of a recognition, where I can recognise that I am recognised by God.

In the voice of Sequeri

(As in previous chapters, the different wavelength of this concluding section has two aims: to summarise Sequeri's thought more simply and also to translate it into modes of expression that are not necessarily his.)

The Irish poet, Patrick Kavanagh, begins a poem entitled 'Advent' with these words: 'we have tested and tasted too much', adding that 'through a chink too wide there comes in no wonder'. Similarly, much thinking on faith has been sepa-rated from the experience of trying to live as believers. Theolo-gians thought that they had to accept the agenda of an empirical philosophy and defend the existence of God in ways that would convince a scientific mentality. But frequently the image of God turned out to be some Big Zeus rather than the

God of Christian revelation. This approach, which can still dominate aggressive television debates about religion, was 'too wide' for real wonder. Wide of the mark in fact. It defended faith but with one hand tied behind its back, in the sense that it lacked the courage to speak about the core of revelation or the depths of religious experience. It paid practically no attention to the human adventure of believing. We have to insist again and again that faith is so much bigger than any talk about the existence of God.

A chink for revelation

So another wavelength is needed if we are to move from the narrowly rational to the genuinely relational and in particular to the birthplace of trust. Take the example of an ordinary conversation between acquaintances. They may know one another from working together. More often than not their communication can remain factual or jocose or safely on the surface. But one day another door opens. A more personal revelation happens. The whole communication is changed by this 'chink' of new honesty or vulnerability, when a spark of trust ignites the relationship. A different mutual appreciation can be born. Such a transformation is an everyday miracle. And this breakthrough into human faith offers us our best parallel for Christian faith. Relationship is more central than rationality for both levels of faith. In both a sense of intuitive rightness takes over from any approach of cautious testing. In both there is a call to emerge from the world of self into a surprising voyage of trusting.

A faith map for today needs that deepening of the agenda. It may even be necessary to go on the offensive in order to defend the everyday validity of faith, whether human or religious. It is time to question the credentials of post-modern agnosticism, which presents itself as so obvious and neutral, and as the accepted position of any liberal democracy. It presumes that there has to be a total split between our verifiable knowing and our personal believing. But what if this assumption is both distorted and dangerous? It takes for granted that there is an unbridgeable gulf between 'objective' and 'subjective'. It ignores something that lies at the root of our shared humanity – our ordinary, and yet extraordinary, experience of trust. This is the basis of our living together. Perhaps we need to make faith into a verb, as something we do, rather than simply something we accept. If so, some kind of 'faithing' – in the form of mutual recognition and trust – is both the core of our human drama and our highway towards meaning. Trusting is quite simply our deepest kind of knowing.

They tell us that this post-modern moment has begun to take our feelings seriously again. Yes, but in what spirit? Trying to escape from an oppressive rationalism we could fall into an unthinking sentimentalism. The Romantic movement in poetry and thought was certainly an important attempt to resist the bleakness of a new urban society. But what we have inherited from it remains ambiguous. The Gospel gives us a vital measuring rod: by its fruits we will know the tree. What are the fruits of our contemporary excitement about affectivity? The cult of feelings in the culture around us can range from the privatised to the narcissistic. How many films end with a couple going off into the twilight, with music rising in the background? It has become one of the icons or clichés of cinema, but it masks a powerful and questionable ideology. Think of the dance at the end of *Slumdog Millionaire*: charming, uplifting, but ultimately escapist. This closing sequence managed to forget the stark suffering of the early part of the film. As in *Titanic*, the audience is sent out feeling good; but cheaply so. We are a long way from *King Lear* or Dostoevsky or Ian McEwan. There are many such examples of short-term sentiment usurping the place of genuine feelings.

The Thomas Revolution

If faith involves feelings, they prove authentic only if they bear fruit in action and in love. At the core of Christian faith is a recognition that God recognises us and comes towards us in the person of Jesus. Think of St Thomas (the doubting one) when, after a week of sulky resistance, he comes face to face with the Risen Christ, and is invited even to touch the wounds. What happens in that moment that leads him to exclaim, 'My Lord and My God'? There had been a deep mutual friendship between them, but now something else is born. His master from Galilee, who died on a cross, is now seen to be alive. A new reality explodes within Thomas, an extraordinary insight about Jesus and about their whole relationship. A moment of recognition has changed everything, literally everything.

This is also a moment when a powerful convergence comes together: affectivity (did Thomas perhaps weep more from fullness than from sorrow?); freedom (his words imply a decision to embrace a different level of discipleship); beauty (glimpsing a glory that has overcome death). This is truth with a difference. It involves what T. S. Eliot called 'a moment in and out of time'. In this instant of joyful upheaval, faith is born. Thomas's dawning perception leads him, not just to a revolutionary new understanding, but to a new love and commitment. It involves not just an intellectual perception but an explosive set of feelings. Notice the word 'my': Jesus is recognised as his Lord and his God. Indeed it is the only time in the Gospels that we have such a declaration. Here the previous human adventure of mutual trust and affection (the core of anthropology) expands into Faith with a capital F (the core of Christology). The Love that is God has undergone death for him, and is standing wounded and transformed before his friend Thomas. Here we are taken beyond any logic that makes sense in a narrowly rational culture. Here truth and affectivity become twins and guide us to a threshold of divine disclosure.

Until we discover the human validity of this kind of knowing, we can remain victims of the narrow models dominant around us. Just as in special experiences of interpersonal trust, the encounter with Christ Risen releases our reason from cramped 'objectivity', allowing it to discover its fullest and most exalted scope. To do justice to a graced and contemplative source of faith, our picture of knowing needs to make room for desire and imagination, for ranges of our humanity that go beyond the measurable in order to meet mystery. It is in line with the celebrated statement of Pascal that the heart has its reasons of which reason knows nothing.

Such an encounter rescues our affectivity from being imprisoned in the private. It invites us to overcome the blinkers of Romanticism and to understand that faith is born from being recognised, and from recognising that you have been recognised. When that happens in human relationships, emotions of trust and gratitude awaken, and the same can be real in religious faith. Go back to Thomas before the Risen Christ to ground and test these claims. His meeting with a truth, greater than he ever imagined possible, rescues him from being an obstinate observer insisting on verification and liberates him into interpersonal amazement. His new vision explodes all his previous expectations. Here deep feeling and an enlarged rationality discover that they are companions. The attitude needed is not that of the laboratory but of the potential lover. The Thomas transformation is perfectly in tune with Flannery O'Connor's remark about a 'blasting annihilating light, a blast that will last a lifetime'.

References to works of Pierangelo Sequeri

All translations from Italian are my own.

DA   *Il Dio Affidabile*, Brescia, 1996.
ED   *L'Estro di Dio: saggi di estetica,* Milan, 2000.
IC   *Interrogazioni sul Cristianesimo* (with Vattimo and Ruggieri), Rome, 2000.
IF   *L'Idea della Fede*, Milan, 2002.
SS   *Sensibili allo Spirito*, Milan, 2001.
SVI   *Senza volgersi indietro*, Milan, 2000.

RE   Anthony J. Kelly, *The Resurrection Effect*, New York, 2008.

10

Joseph Ratzinger: God with a human face

The week after Pope Benedict XVI was elected in April 2005, the sale of books by Joseph Ratzinger on Amazon.com soared, so much so that he ousted *The Da Vinci Code* from first place. But one may wonder how many of the books were read in full by those enthusiastic buyers. In common with other thinkers explored in these pages, Ratzinger is a complex and scholarly author, as will be seen from the overview of his thinking on faith offered here. Our first section will draw on his writings before his election as Pope and a second part will outline major points of continuity between his publications before April 2005 and his reflections on faith since becoming the successor of St Peter.

Critique of contemporary culture

1 April 2005 is a significant date from which to start. On that evening Cardinal Ratzinger was at Subiaco, the historic Benedictine foundation outside Rome, in order to receive a special award. It was the night before the death of John Paul II, and Cardinal Ratzinger gave an in-depth lecture entitled 'Europe's Crisis of Culture', offering a fairly negative diagnosis of the continent today. In his view, its dominant culture offers a 'radical contradiction not only of Christianity but of the religious and moral traditions of humanity' (*EPB*, 328). He went on to say that our moral energy has not kept pace with our technical power, that God is now tolerated only in the private areas of existence, and ultimately that Europe, by forgetting its Christian history, risks becoming like a dried up tree without roots. Although the Enlightenment was of Christian origin, and enshrined important values of rationality, it has now degenerated into dogmatic relativism. Its self-sufficient version of reason seems a danger to humanity. By contrast Christianity can be seen 'as the religion of the Logos, as the religion according to reason', where creative reason is ultimately revealed as love 'in the crucified God' (*EPB*, 333–4). Faced with this clash of two different

visions of life, we need people of 'enlightened and lived faith' like St. Benedict, who, in 'a time of dissipation and decadence', had the spiritual resources to make faith credible again (*EPB*, 335).

By any account this was a remarkable lecture, but it assumes special importance because it was Cardinal Ratzinger's last discourse of this kind before his election as Pope. It also brings together some of the principal insights that he had explored for years: his concern about an increasingly secular Europe, where faith seems ousted from public life, where religious traditions seem more and more fragile, and where a shrunken rationality has created, as he said two weeks later, 'the dictatorship of relativism, which does not recognize anything as certain'. This expression came in his pre-conclave homily, in which he evoked the confusions suffered by believers today, thrown around 'from collectivism to radical individualism; from atheism to a vague religious mysticism'. And he went on to state one of his oft-repeated perspectives on faith: 'In Christ truth and love coincide ... in our own life truth and love merge (*EPB*, 22–3). A decade earlier, in Mexico, he had voiced a parallel position (and one to which we will return): 'Reason will not be saved without the faith, but the faith without reason will not be human' (*EPB*, 239).

Those two texts of April 2005 offered a somewhat dark picture of the faith situation. 'Dialectical' is a label sometimes applied to the theology of Cardinal Ratzinger, and with some justification. He tends to see faith more in opposition to the 'world' than in dialogue with it. In particular, he sees the inheritance of modernity as having produced a set of influences, intellectual and social, hostile to religion. 'A Christianity that believes it has no other function than to be completely in tune with the spirit of the times has nothing to say and no meaning to offer' (*PCT*, 57). In this light theologians who see faith as easily compatible with this modern inheritance risk falling into naïve progressivism. Ratzinger prefers to critique those traits of the culture that undermine the possibility of faith: pragmatism leaves little room for contemplative receptivity; individualist autonomy tends to a one-sided view of freedom and stifles the need for salvation; a narrow rationalism has no time for mystery; a merely empirical approach leaves no space for wonder and imprisons the self in the here and now; alienation from

tradition leaves people without anchors in their search for meaning; exaggerating the socio-political relevance of Christianity can
reduce faith to ideology and activism; and post-modern relativism
questions the very possibility of truth. Suffering from the burden of
so much complexity, we can easily be attracted by a mood of
resigned indifference or agnosticism that masquerades as openness
or tolerance. It was significant that when Ratzinger was named
Archbishop of Munich in 1977, he took as his motto a phrase
from St Paul, *cooperatores veritatis*, co-workers for the truth.

A more positive and pastoral tone

If his verdict on contemporary culture appears severe or even
antagonistic, that does not constitute the whole of Ratzinger's
theology about belief today. He has pondered at length how the
understanding and the expression of faith should be renewed for
the needs of today. The positive vision that emerges here balances
his more critical judgements on the culture. Basic to his vision is
the biblical notion of exodus: a person of faith, like Abraham, is
called to go beyond self in a movement that comes from God. Just
as God as Trinity is not a solitary deity but relational in love,
believers live their own 'ecstasy' or movement towards God and
others in love. It is striking that Cardinal Ratzinger, although for
many years Prefect of the Congregation for the Doctrine of the
Faith, did not give much attention to doctrine in his more pastoral
reflections on faith today. Existential, spiritual and ecclesial dimensions were more central for him.

Less than six months before he was elected Pope, in a lengthy
interview with a liberal Italian newspaper, he described faith in
terms that foreshadow what he was to write in his first encyclical.
'The true essence of Christianity', he said, 'is a love story between
God and human beings. If one could understand this in the
language of today, everything else would follow' (*La Repubblica*,
19 November 2004). He went on to say that an intellectual presen-
tation of faith, while important, cannot meet the more existential
challenges of today. Instead, people need living spaces of community and of growth together. 'Only through concrete experiences
and existential witness is it possible to make the Christian message

accessible and real today'. And he added that 'faith is not only the fruit of tradition' but is 'the outcome of a free yes to Christ from one's heart'.

This more open and exploratory tone is not the Ratzinger pictured by the mass media, either before his election as Pope or in more recent controversies that can easily eclipse his spiritual explorations of faith. And yet to create a fresh language, free from the dullness of older expressions, has been the underlying motivation of all his work: 'My basic impulse, precisely during the Council, was always to free up the authentic kernel of the faith from encrustations and to give this kernel strength and dynamism. This impulse is the constant of my life' (*SE*, 79).

An ecclesial reality

This chapter seeks to focus on Ratzinger's theology of faith and it will not try to do justice to other important themes in his work (such as morality, liturgy, biblical studies, eschatology or the Second Vatican Council). We are asking, as in other chapters of this book, what we can learn from him in order to construct a map towards faith for today. Perhaps we can summarise Ratzinger's pastoral approach under three headings. He presents faith as a) an ecclesial and sacramental reality; b) as a unity of love and ultimate meaning; and c) as a source of both purification and joy.

A central passion of Joseph Ratzinger's life, as theologian and now as Pope, has been to communicate the credibility of faith for today's world, often by drawing on the riches of the first millennium. Aware that we live in a context no longer supportive of religion, he emphasises faith as both decision and developing commitment. Today's believers need the courage to be countercultural, and so the nourishing of adult faith becomes central. Because faith involves an alternative way of life, different to that promoted by the dominant culture, Ratzinger has often praised committed Christian communities or movements as emerging forms of church for today.

For him the Church should be not only 'a place of experience' but 'a source of new personal experience' (*PCT*, 351), where people learn how to become disciples of Christ within today's culture. A crucial challenge, in his view, is to create life-experiences that can bring the treasures of tradition alive again. At the origin of the conversion of the ancient world was 'an invitation from experience to experience' (*LC*, 36) where the early Christians attracted others to share their encounter with the Risen Lord. It is still true that 'education in the faith is unthinkable without a believing community' (*PCT*, 128). Such communities can help people to take a stand in the cultural battleground of today: 'the whole of history is marked by this strange dilemma between the silent, gentle claim of truth and the urgent pressure of utility' (*LC*, 28).

One of Ratzinger's favourite expressions is 'the we-structure of faith' (*PCT*, 15). Just as the Christian God is revealed as a Trinitarian 'we' or communion of persons, so Christian faith is encountered through relationship with the Church. The 'I believe' of faith moves from the personal to the 'we believe' of the Church's communal worship of God. Although 'faith is a supremely personal act', each person is a receiver rather than a maker, who needs a living tradition: 'the "we" of the church is the new communion into which God draws us beyond our narrow selves' (*EPB*, 212–13). It is here that faith is born and nourished through 'the memory of the Church' (*PCT*, 23). The personalism of an I-Thou relationship with God is important, but it needs to root itself in an experience of memory, of community, of the great 'we' of tradition. Ultimately faith cannot be 'something thought up by me' but rather 'a call to community', the community of the Word (*IC*, 58–9).

If faith starts from experience, that experience is best captured in the progress of catechumens towards adult baptism. This involves 'a long learning process' which culminates in the question and answer dialogue of the sacrament, expressing the 'call and the acceptance' structure of faith (*PCT*, 34–5). In this way, the catechumens learn to die to themselves and discover that life can be a going out of oneself (*ekstatis*) with Christ. More than most theologians, Ratzinger's reflection on faith pays attention to the liturgical aspects of church life. It is here that faith becomes a *paideia*, a school of life and of love. He told a gathering of catechists, who had come to Rome for the Jubilee Year of 2000, that evangelisation means showing people faith as an 'art of living'. He added that our liturgical celebrations can be too rationalist, as if the main aim were intelligibility; instead our worship needs to cultivate more silence, more beauty and a prayerful sense of mystery.

Side by side with Ratzinger's stress on the ecclesial dimension of faith is his insistence on the Church as servant of faith. She should never become an end in herself, because a mirror that reflects only itself is no longer a mirror. Instead the Church exists to mediate and make Christ known, and as she encounters different moments of history, her institutions are always in need of discernment and self-examination.

Logos becomes Love

This communitarian dimension is accompanied and balanced by an emphasis on personal spirituality and on the drama of doubt in today's world. The opening chapter of Joseph Ratzinger's best known book, *Introduction to Christianity*, plunges the reader into an evocation of the modern crisis of faith. In these pages, published in the symbolic year of 1968, the crisis is depicted not in terms of ideas, but as a struggle with doubt in a period when faith can often seem impossible. The preacher is portrayed as feeling like a foreigner in the current culture or sounding like a relic from the past. Ratzinger then reminds his readers of the perennial vulnerability of faith. 'The believer is always threatened with uncertainty' (*IC*, 17). More forcefully still he writes: 'both the believer and the unbeliever share, each in his own way, doubt *and* belief' (*IC*, 21).

In a book of interviews, published in 2000, he said that as long as faith is a pilgrim in this life, it will experience moments of fragility. Even a Pope, he remarked, can suffer from difficulties and darkness. 'Faith is always a path', never a convenient ideology, but it can mature by confronting 'the oppression and the power of unbelief' (*GW*, 36–7). Have we then left behind forever the securities of an age of faith, as in the Middle Ages? Ratzinger wonders aloud how many people in the past 'really entered into the movement of belief' (*IC*, 23) and he insists that genuine faith 'has always been a decision' involving a transformation of the believer (*IC*, 25).

How can we describe the experience of faith? Ratzinger proposes that it is a way of trustfully depending on the word of God and that this 'cannot be reduced to knowledge' (*IC*, 42). It implies a disposition of openness, where we recognise our need of a gift. To know God is not mainly a question of thinking but of encountering a revelation. And he sees this in counter-cultural terms: 'the primacy of the invisible over the visible and that of receiving over making runs directly counter' to contemporary assumptions (*IC*, 43–4). The personal encounter at the root of faith is with 'the human being Jesus', but it is through Him that we experience 'the meaning of the world as person' (*IC*, 47).

However, an existential interpretation of faith as trust can remain one-sided. In tune with St Bonaventure, who insisted on a connection between love and truth, Ratzinger remains keen to emphasise the truth dimension of faith. Because truth and love are united in Christ, Logos and Love are now inseparable: 'the meaning of the world is present before us as love which loves even me' (*IC*, 48). Hence we should not exaggerate the distinction between the God of philosophy and of faith, or the difference between rationality and relationship. But the truth of faith is one that we receive rather than create or possess. Ratzinger sees as uniquely Christian the enlargement of the Greek idea of *logos* in the Fourth Gospel: 'The *logos* of the whole world ... is at the same time love' (*IC*, 103). These core insights will return as central in Pope Benedict's first encyclical.

On this basis Ratzinger always resisted tendencies to water down the truth claims of Christianity. Just as Newman fought the 'liberalism' of his age, Ratzinger battled with various forms of relativism, and remains deeply suspicious of any separation of faith as love from faith as truth. Under the banner of open-mindedness even believers can become anonymous agnostics, accepting that truth is impossible, and so they can fall for a woolly version of Christianity as a vague religion of love.

Toughness and beauty

'The very toughness of the adventure is what makes it beautiful' (*FF*, 75). On the one hand, the Christian travels a purifying road, marked by a life-long struggle against deception and sin. On the other, faith is a source of lightness and of joy, because the burden of making sense of ourselves is lifted when we walk in the presence of the Risen Lord.

In various speeches on faith and culture, Cardinal Ratzinger adapted a saying of St Basil about the prophet Amos being a cutter of sycamores. This tree, it seems, produces its best sap when one cuts into its bark, and this becomes an image of the purifying impact of faith on human cultures. And the same is true of individuals. 'Prophetic salt' burns and changes us in order to make us more 'constant in the Yes' (*PCT*, 57, 64). Faith is never a finished business to be taken for granted. It has to be 'constantly renewed' because it involves 'a perishing of the mere self and a resurrection of the true self' (*EPB*, 211–12). But this purifying process, which is part of the Christian journey, should not be reduced to moralism or to Gospel 'values': any genuinely Christian 'no' has its place only within the greater and graced 'yes' of a relational faith.

'To believe is to be granted a share in Jesus's vision' (*EPB*, 213), he 'whose human vision of the divine reality is the source of light for everyone' (*LC*, 32). Ratzinger has claimed, not without causing some controversy, that 'faith' is an exclusively Christian phenomenon: because of the uniqueness of the revelation of God in Jesus Christ, believing in him is the key to the nature of 'faith' (*LC*, 10). In this light he has remained critical of oriental spiritualities as impersonal searching, which lacks a prayerful relationship with the God who transforms us. Genuine faith exists where God speaks to us and calls us into divine love. When that invitation is accepted, meditation means not only a form of quiet attentiveness but a response to a gift of new life in Christ. Thus faith views our human journey as the theatre of God's continuing work as creator and redeemer.

The Christian vision, according to Ratzinger, can claim to be 'more optimistic and more radical' than the dominant culture of today (*PCT*, 338). A believer enjoys a certain 'lightness' of heart that gives consolation even in situations of confusion or emptiness, and ultimately in the face of death. These fruits of the Spirit do not depend on human effort but rather on God's initiative. On this point Ratzinger seems to echo Balthasar: 'I can know only because I am known, love only because I am already loved' and then he adds his own particular note: such 'confidence and trust' are 'possible in this world only because the ground of being is trustworthy' (*PCT*, 74).

A final pastoral perspective to close this pre-papal section. On various occasions Cardinal Ratzinger commented on the meeting of Jesus with the Samaritan woman in John's Gospel as an example of development towards mature faith. At the end of this episode the townspeople say that they now believe, 'no longer because of what you told us' but because they have heard and known for themselves. The future Pope saw this as passing from 'second-hand' to 'firsthand' faith, because it now involves 'a personal encounter with the Lord' (*PCT*, 351). Especially today faith needs to become a recognition or 'knowledge' of this kind (*LC*, 34). To guide people towards such a threshold of discovery remains, in his view, the aim of all faith formation.

After April 2005

There is a clear continuity between Cardinal Ratzinger's earlier writings in theology and his many explorations of faith as Pope. Speaking to the Catholic University of America in Washington in April 2008, Pope Benedict acknowledged the 'reluctance many people have today in entrusting themselves to God', adding that it 'is a complex phenomenon and one which I ponder continually' (17 April 2008). This is a revealingly personal comment and one that shows that a key concern of his pontificate is to make faith real for a secular world.

On more than one occasion he has quoted his own theological work. Speaking to a symposium of university professors in June 2008, he took a sentence from *Introduction to Christianity*: 'Christian faith has made its clear choice: against the gods of religion for the God of philosophers', adding that this was 'a deep conviction which I have expressed many times'. He went on to insist that this basic link between Christian faith and philosophical reflection did not imprison faith within a world of theory, but instead saved it from being cut off from the realm of truth' (Address to the Sixth European Symposium for University Professors, 7 June 2008). A few months later, during his visit to Paris, he returned to another major topic of his, commenting that 'God has truly become for many the great unknown' and that when a positivistic culture drives the search for God into the private sphere, it is 'a disaster for humanity' (Address to representatives of the world of culture, 12 September 2008).

In this light the remainder of this chapter will summarise, under seven headings, a number of recurring themes in the discourses of Pope Ratzinger (a term commonly and respectfully used in Italian).

Enlarging the agenda of rationality

A frequent concern has been to rescue rationality from the various shrunken forms of rationalism in the post-Enlightenment world. The Pope views this as an anthropological crisis – a question of how we see ourselves – rather than simply a matter of philosophy or theology. Just as a human being is always more than can be examined empirically, 'truth means more than knowledge'. Religious truth, in particular is essentially personal and speaks to the whole of our humanity 'inviting us to respond with our whole being' (Catholic University of America, Washington DC, 17 April 2008).

Similarly, a human being is always more than can be examined empirically: 'truth means more than knowledge.' Religious truth, in particular is essentially personal and speaks to the whole of our humanity 'inviting us to respond with our whole being' (Catholic University of America, Washington DC, 17 April 2008).'

St Augustine once remarked that knowledge on its own may produce only sadness. Therefore, 'knowing God is not enough ... Knowledge must become love' (Pontifical Gregorian University, Rome, 3 November 2006). To enlarge the conversation about reason and faith is one of the keys to what Pope Benedict calls (echoing Rosmini) a ministry of intellectual charity.

Faith as fragile and gradual.

Joseph Ratzinger as theologian had often acknowledged the struggles that are part of the human experience of faith. More recently, speaking off-the-cuff to Roman seminarians, the Pope described the gradualism of the journey of faith in these terms: 'I found Augustine's great humanity fascinating, because from the outset as a catechumen he was simply unable to identify with the Church, but instead had to have a spiritual struggle to find, little by little, access to the Word of God, to life with God' (17 February 2007).

In this same spirit, at the end of his annual Christmas meeting with the Roman Curia in December 2009, he used a striking image to evoke the situation of those who search for spiritual meaning but cannot find themselves at home in the church as they perceive it. Referring to the episode when Jesus banished merchants from the Temple, so that it could be 'a house of prayer for all the nations', the Pope commented that Jesus wanted to restore the 'so-called Court-yard of the Gentiles' to its proper purpose as 'a free space for the Gentiles who wished to pray there to the one God, even if they could not take part in the mystery'. Agnostics or atheists of today, he added, can be 'taken aback' when we 'speak of a new evangelisa-tion': they do not want to 'see themselves as an object of mission'. And Pope Benedict went on to make an imaginative proposal: 'I think that today too the Church should open a sort of "Courtyard of the Gentiles" in which people might in some way latch on to God, without knowing him and before gaining access to his mys-tery' (Address to the Roman Curia, 21 December 2009).

Social fruits of faith

When, in October 1998, Cardinal Ratzinger took part in a sympo-sium to honour the 70th birthday of Johann Baptist Metz, a leading proponent of 'political theology', he ended his lecture with these words: 'the question of God is finally not a theoretical question, but rather the question of the *praxis* of one's life' (*ET*, 25). In spite of his reservations about an excessively Marxist influence in liberation theology, he had always spoken out against the scandal of poverty and in favour of believers struggling against injustice. Even before the strong social vision of his third encyclical, *Caritas in veritate*, his second such letter had stated: 'The Christian message is not only "informative" but "performative". 'The Gospel is not merely a communication of things that can be known – it makes things happen and is life-changing" (*SS*, §2).

Discernment of culture

The picture of life promoted by the dominant 'cultural images' around us can induce a 'practical denial of God', a situation where there is 'no longer any need for God' (Address to the Pontifical Council for Culture, 8 March 2008). In a consumerist context, faith needs to be presented 'in an engaging and imaginative way, to a society which markets any number of recipes for human fulfil-ment' (Meeting with Bishops of the United States of America, 16 April 2008). Hence believers will need new skills to discern light from darkness in the many messages that bombard us today.

Modernity was founded on two pillars, a new sense of freedom and a new sense of reason. Gradually, however, these achievements have revealed their shadow sides and the challenges remain with us today: 'we face two poles: on the one hand, subjective arbitrariness, and on the other, fundamentalist fanaticism'. But deep in each person lies the intuition 'that at the beginning of all things, there must be not irrationality, but creative Reason – not blind chance, but freedom' (Address to representatives of the world of culture, Paris, 12 September 2008).

Faith as response to love as truth

Pope Benedict's first encyclical surprised many people with its eloquent hymn to love (as *The Times* described it). The opening spoke of faith as rooted in a decision that responds to a gift: 'not an ethical choice or a lofty idea, but the encounter with an event, a person, which gives life a new horizon' where 'love is not a com-mand but a response to … God who draws near to us' (*DCE*, § 1). Any facile interpretation is countered by the Pope's third encycli-cal, where he warns that love runs a fatal risk of becoming divorced from truth. If so, it 'degenerates into sentimentality' like 'an empty shell, to be filled in an arbitrary way' (*CinV*, § 3).

Uniqueness of Christ: Logos as incarnate love

As seen in his earlier writings, Pope Benedict speaks of the novelty of the Gospel not in terms of an idea, but a person – 'the figure of Christ himself' gives to Christianity 'an unprecedented realism'

(*DCE*, § 12). As Pope, he has continued to explore the idea of Logos as a key to the truth of Christ. In 1998, he linked a high vision of the Creative Logos with the healing presence of Christ: when people 'cannot find the way to God on their own', the Shepherd who carries them home is 'the Logos itself, the eternal Word, the eternal meaning of the cosmos that dwells in the Son of Man' (*ET*, 21). Exactly this same insight is found in his first encyclical, where reason and love unite: 'this universal principle of creation – the *Logos*, primordial reason – is at the same time a lover with all the passion of a true love' (*DCE*, § 10).

Faith and reason: mutual purification

'Faith liberates reason from its blind spots and therefore helps it to be ever more fully itself' (*DCE*, § 28). Less than a year after that first encyclical, this was again a main concern in the Pope Benedict's lecture at the University of Regensburg, which proposed a 'broadening of our concept of reason'. The irrational controversy that arose after this speech was all the more ironic because one of its central themes was the need to protect both faith and reason from extremism, by having them 'come together in a new way'. The lecture acknowledged that sickness can infect both reason and relation: 'this is a dangerous state of affairs for humanity, as we see from the disturbing pathologies of religion and reason which necessarily erupt when reason is so reduced that questions of religion and ethics no longer concern it' (Regensburg lecture, 12 September 2006).

Although the Regensburg university discourse attracted much comment, few noticed that earlier on that same day the Pope had treated the same theme in a homily. After evoking the modern challenges to faith, he repeated his emphasis on the Logos: 'We believe that at the beginning of everything is the eternal Word, with Reason and not Unreason'. He went on to touch on another of his constant themes about Christian revelation, whereby the Logos becomes incarnate love: 'This creative Reason is Goodness, it is Love. It has a face. God does not leave us groping in the dark'. A little later came a passage that deserves quoting at more length, since it captured so much of the Pope's vision: 'Today, when we have learned to recognize the pathologies and the life-threatening diseases associated with religion and reason, and the ways that God's image can be destroyed by hatred and fanaticism, it is important to state clearly the God in whom we believe, and to proclaim confidently that this God has a human face. Only this can free us from being afraid of God – which is ultimately at the root of modern atheism' (Homily at Mass, Islinger Feld, Regensburg, 12 September 2006). Particularly striking are the claims that atheism originates from false fear of a false God, and that in the Incarnation of God lies our Christian way of saving religion and reason from their potential distortions.

Conclusion

What are some of the contributions of Pope Benedict to our cumulative faith map? Much more than other thinkers, he seeks to defend faith as a religion of Logos, grounded in reason. This is not the narrow reason inherited from the Enlightenment or from scientism, or from an older apologetics, but rather the full range of human rationality, embracing thinking, feeling, existential options and prayerfulness. He wants a reflective faith for today to root itself in a sense of the creative reason that is God, and which shows itself to us as in Jesus Christ.

If this can seem rather intellectual, in fact Ratzinger has devoted himself to translating this high vision into more spiritual and pastoral language. Rather like Newman, whom he greatly admires, he wants to deepen our sense of the human person as ready for God's Word. He frequently speaks of the Abraham-like journey of faith as an exodus from the ego or even as an ecstasy of standing outside one's small self. As we have seen, he connects this adventure of faith with liturgy and, in particular, with the baptismal initiation of catechumens. In his view the best faith map, so to speak, comes from witnessing the Christian experience alive in other people. By glimpsing a fullness of life as embodied in the saints, canonised or unknown, a decision of faith becomes more possible for the mind and the heart.

The pressures and confusions of today's culture mean that faith has to be actively critical, not simply by unmasking reductive ideas and life-styles, but rather by creating alternative communities and ways of life. Faith should not allow itself to appear negative, because it is grounded in a great Yes to God and to life, which originates in God's Yes to us. A believer is blessed with consolation about ultimate meaning as love. In spite of the darkness that faith can encounter, it takes its stand on the promise of God's own fidelity and this remains, in every age, its unique strength.

A final characteristic quotation can be taken from Pope Benedict's first 'Urbi et Orbi' Christmas message: 'The modern age is often seen as an awakening of reason from its slumbers, humanity's enlightenment after an age of darkness. Yet without the light of Christ, the light of reason is not sufficient to enlighten humanity and the world' (Urbi et Orbi address, 24 December 2005).

References to works of Joseph Ratzinger

EPB *The Essential Pope Benedict XVI, His Central Writings and Speeches*, ed. J. F. Thornton & S. B. Varenne, San Francisco, 2007.

FF *Faith and the Future*, Chicago, 1971.

GW *God and the World* (conversation with Peter Seewald), San Francisco, 2002.

IC *Introduction to Christianity*, London, 1969.

LC *To Look on Christ: Exercises in Faith, Hope and Love*, Slough, 1991.

SE *The Salt of the Earth* (Interviews with Peter Seewald), San Francisco, 1997.

PCT *Principles of Catholic Theology: Building Stones for a Fundamental Theology*, San Francisco, 1987.

ET *The End of Time? The Provocation of Talking about God*, with J. B. Metz *et al.*, ed. J. M. Ashley, New York, 2004.

DCE *Deus caritas est*, Encyclical Letter, 2005.

SS *Spe Salvi*, Encyclical Letter, 2007

CinV *Caritas in Veritate*, Encyclical Letter, 2009

Conclusion:
Converging pillars of wisdom

In 2009, the Canadian novelist Margaret Atwood published *The Year of the Flood*, a grim satire on our capacity for self-destruction, set in a post-apocalyptic world of the future. What is fascinating is the religious dimension of the novel, where an ecological group called 'God's Gardeners' live in counter-cultural communes. Each of the book's thirteen sections begins with a sermon from their leader and with an environmentally correct hymn. These seem both brilliantly credible and tongue-in-cheek. What is the significance of all this religiousness or all these biblical references? Is it just nostalgic or is this novel evoking redemption or forgiveness, with its final moment of music 'winding towards us through the darkness'? Why all this mention of God in what is basically an agnostic narrative? Or is it rather a gnostic text, in the sense of a drifting spirituality without object, without definite faith? Flannery O'Connor would possibly accuse Atwood of playing with catastrophe but having no roots or commitment.

Desire and uncertainty

I think a more compassionate interpretation is possible. Margaret Atwood manages to capture where our culture finds itself: spiritually adrift most of the time, longing for something more, yet often remaining uncertain and afraid. In this sense she dramatises the fragility of faith today. This is embodied in the principal character of Toby, a woman who rises to high office in the Gardeners but never fully accepts their vision. When she is invited to accept a new leadership role she says, 'I'm not sure I believe in all of it'. To which the leader, Adam One, replies, 'In some religions, faith precedes action. In ours, action precedes faith ... We should not expect too much from faith ... Any religion is a shadow of God. But the shadows of God are not God'. The text is studded with comments about spiritual truth being absurd from a materialist point of view or with quotations from Julian of Norwich that 'everything has its being through the love of God'.

Perhaps more important than these religious pointers is the whole process of reading this story. The reader's experience is one of double consciousness, of sympathy and distance, of attraction for the spiritual vision, but unease with the naivety of it all in a tragically violent world. In this way the book embodies something of the spiritual imagination of our time, its longing to believe but its paralysis on the threshold of faith. Established traditions of religion seem too simple for this problematic world. Their wisdom remains attractive but unreachable. It recalls Rahner's diagnosis of a threshold stance of desire, accompanied by an incapacity for decision. Within a culture of fragmentation Atwood recognises a deep hunger for God and a longing for some salvation. But she keeps a satiric distance from any concrete foundations of religiousness beyond the personal.

A similar but stronger scepticism was discernible in one of the successful films of 2009, *A serious man*, directed by the Coen brothers. In a specifically Jewish context, we revisit the story of Job in modern and comic form. Larry is a physics professor, an expert in quantum mechanics and the uncertainty principle, who is assaulted by a series of misfortunes. Why have we questions if there are no answers, he asks. The rabbis he consults offer little more than platitudes. 'Accept the mystery' seems to be the only response. The world is capricious and God unknowable. You resist nihilism with courage and comedy, with a lingering sense that there has to be some purpose, but don't expect any steady light or consolation. This film seems more dark and disillusioned than Atwood's novel, but together they represent a tone that is typical of now. Religious questions are alive, even though the answers on offer are hard to credit.

An initial triangle

If Atwood and the Coens capture something of our spiritual sensibility, what have we learned from the ten perspectives of this book that can even begin to meet that world? For the most part, our authors were responding to an earlier moment in cultural history. They had in mind the more definite unbelief of modernity rather than the indefinite quest of post-modernity. Have they anything to offer to the new spiritual searchers? How can their reflections be translated for those who inhabit Pope Benedict's 'Courtyard of the Gentiles', those whom he recognised as allergic to institutional religion but as wondering about an Unknown God? In this conclusion I hope to suggest some bridges between the wisdom discovered in our previous chapters and the emerging sensibility of our twenty-first century.

In his famous 1927 book, *The Mystical Element of Religion*, Friedrich von Hügel saw three dimensions of religion as connected with childhood, youth and adulthood. Children can grow up happily within an 'institutional' kind of faith, where their images of life are shaped by their belonging to a church tradition. A young person then runs into new questions and needs a more 'critical' approach: now one's interpretation of life needs to find reasons that make sense. For von Hügel a third or adult stage of faith goes beyond the institutional and the rational dimensions to a more 'mystical' phase. By this he meant that religion will need to be experienced in depth, to be felt rather 'than seen or reasoned about' and to be 'loved and lived rather than analyzed'.

Von Hügel saw these three dimensions not only as chronological stages but also as essential to a gradual maturity of faith: starting from fidelity to the church, facing questions and searching for answers, and experiencing a personal depth of spiritual surrender. The 'institutional' dimension is meant to give us a place of belonging where we receive God's revelation. The 'critical' element offers us tools of intellectual inquiry into the validity and significance of faith. The 'mystical' dimension nourishes a more personal and profound encounter with grace. Von Hügel sums up his vision in one concise sentence: 'I believe because I am told, because it is true, because it answers to my deepest interior experiences and needs'.

All three dimensions – of community and head and heart – can and should live together in healthy tension. If the institutional element dominates, religion can become externally loyalist, and forgetful of that deep trust 'in a person towards a Person'. If intellectual reflection takes over, we risk neglecting the need for community and affectivity. If interior spirituality monopolises the agenda, it can evade the fragile reality of a human Church and the perennial limitations of human understanding.

Towards seven pillars of wisdom

This triangle of von Hügel provides a fruitful entry point to key dimensions of faith, but for today and in the light of our previous chapters, his three points of emphasis need to be supplemented. I propose four other horizons that can add up to 'seven pillars of wisdom' (to echo a famous expression of the Book of Proverbs). To begin with let us revisit von Hügel's triangle, translating it into a different idiom, seeking at each step to address those who live a typically postmodern spiritual quest.

First pillar: The wisdom of belonging

> The Church is vast enough to contain
> the greatest minds, and the most diverse.
> Henri de Lubac

Faith is not a solo run. Each of our ten thinkers developed their vision within the tradition of meaning that is the Church – some more painfully than others. In spite of everything, to echo G. K. Chesterton, the Church can save us from the slavery of being the children only of our own time. It gives us roots in a much longer adventure of light and struggle. This pillar of wisdom involves being-with-others now and also enjoying a rich inheritance from the past. But in today's fragmented culture and with an often wounded image of church, belonging within a religious tradition has become more difficult and more rare. It is an understatement to say that the church is not always experienced as a spiritual home.

Even though you may think of the Church or the Churches with little enthusiasm, or even with deep distrust, ask yourself whether you need to invent the wheel again. In spite of its frightening failures, the Church has been a space of nourishment for countless numbers of people through many centuries. It has developed scaffolding for journeys towards possible faith: through reflection on life and on revelation, through skills of interiority, through sacramental celebration, through the witness of self-giving by ordinary people and by saints. Without some such companionship with believers, the journey towards faith can simply be too lonely and without signposts.

Second pillar: The world of reflection

> All who seek truth seek God,
> whether this is clear to them or not.
> Edith Stein

Are there any major issues about faith that have not been agonised over in the long history of Christian theology? What we found in our ten explorers is a desire to learn from the past in order to rethink the significance of faith for a radically changed context. They were all acutely aware of new difficulties today, usually more cultural than intellectual, more to do with a shift of sensibility than with objections to the creed. All ten set out to deepen or enlarge the agenda. They wanted to revisit Christian faith as a living and liveable reality, at once coherent and personal.

The idea of 'theology' may ring all the wrong bells for you. It can seem a field of hair-splitting irrelevance. But at its best the job of theology has always been to ponder, pray and incarnate God's Word for now, for many different 'nows'. It is an art of the crossroads, standing in-between, receiving a revelation and translating it. Its call is to mediate God's meaning for us.

Quite recently close friends of mine remarked that their small daughter had become a 'specialist in the interrogative'! She had discovered 'What' as in 'what is that?' before moving on to her current favourite word, 'Why?' Such simple words open a whole universe. Questioning expresses, as Lonergan liked to say, the eros of our spirit, our innate drive to know. Concerning faith there are hosts of important questions and a long inheritance of spiritually nourishing answers. Above all enjoy and embrace your questions. You have to let them come alive before the answers can make sense.

Third pillar: The inner drama

> Gather my fragments towards
> the radium, the
> all swallowing moment
> once more.
> Margaret Avison

Prayer, in its many forms, is the key expression of faith. It ranges from the ordinary voicing of prayers to moments of profound silence, sometimes blessed with fullness, sometimes locked in darkness or agony. Think of the gamut of emotions found in the psalms – from confusion to gratitude, from rage to tenderness, and from painful questioning to being filled with hope again.

Christian prayer means relaxing into the reality of being loved by God, in order to rise, each day, into the gritty realism of loving. If it is genuine, it brings about an erosion of the small ego, a slow transformation towards an otherwise unreachable freedom. As Sequeri reminded us, we are invited into the inner space of Christ's own prayer, glimpsing and sharing his trust in Abba-Father.

Perhaps your postmodern sensibility is tempted to look for an inner space of spiritual quiet. There is a fascination today with inner journeys, with meditation methods that aim to put you in touch with the now. So far so good. It touches a felt need of our time, a longing for another quality of life. A best-selling book tells us to become the 'guardians of our inner space' and to 'measure everything by the degree of peace we feel within'. But is this more than an attractive half-truth? It seems to forget the hard work required for any lasting spiritual commitment.

A Christian prayer journey goes further. It will seek for peace 'not as the world gives', and it will surely run into 'many conflicts' as George Herbert said about his poetry. 'The Collar', one of his most famous poems, begins with an outburst of angry frustration and broken lines, only to end with harmony as a surprising gift. It goes from the rebellion of 'I struck the board and cried, No more' to a serene acceptance – arrived at not as achievement but as gift.

> But as I raved and grew more fierce and wild
>   At every word
> Methoughts I heard one calling, Child:
>   And I replied, My Lord.

(By the way, with the hidden subtlety of Herbert, there is probably a triple pun in the title: yoke, choler, caller.)

Overview of the seven wisdoms

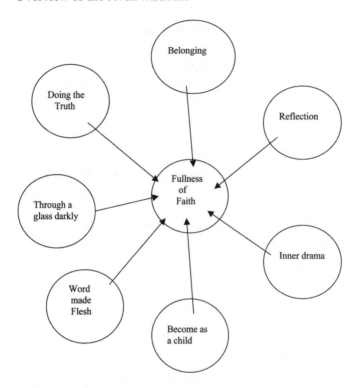

Fourth pillar: 'Unless you become as a child'

> Concepts create idols,
> only wonder really knows.
> Gregory of Nyssa.

G. K. Chesterton was a great defender of the child within the adult, inviting us to embrace a 'godlike imagination which makes all things new'. We already discovered Newman's emphasis on disposition: our openness or closedness to faith is prior to thinking or words. We also saw Flannery O'Connor poking fun at our shields of pride. She wanted to break them down to make us ready for grace.

Those three authors would be alarmed by the self-satisfied externalism of the 'new atheists' of recent years, who simply ignore the fact that faith involves some spiritual preconditions. Without a

spirit of receiving and reverence, we can be like the sullen children
that Jesus satirised in a parable: they neither danced to happy music
nor wept with sad songs. The philosopher Wittgenstein remarked
that it is only love can believe in the Resurrection.

*Attitude is all, but your postmodern self can suffer from too much
tourism and not enough pilgrimage. A New York artist and friend of
mine, Alfonse Borysewicz, created a chapel-like structure some years ago,
entitled 'Your Own Soul'. The outside was covered with numbers and
tears, but there was a small opening into the interior. So you had to go
down on your knees to enter. Once inside at first you saw only a dark
dead body. Then gradually, as your eyes got used to the dimness, small
gold images came into focus. It seemed a parable of faith. If you do not
enter humbly you will not see. If you do not wait in darkness, you will
not find the treasure. As Mary's Magnificat says: the proud will be
scattered in the imagination of their hearts but the hungry will find
nourishment.*

Fifth pillar: The Word Made Flesh

> Christianity teaches discovery.
> Elmar Salmann

Here we come to the core challenge of Christianity, and one that
can provoke unease in the postmodern searcher. It seems far too
definite. That is, and always was, the scandal of the Gospel. Some
agnostic philosophers of today like to speak of the possibility of
God. But here we dare to speak of reality, historic and yet eternal.

There is a major challenge here; not only the truth that God
came among us, but the longer story of God's self-communication
to humanity. Christian faith stands or falls on these claims about
Biblical revelation. The other pillars of wisdom fade into vagueness
if God has not spoken to us.

All the ten 'giants' of previous chapters agree on this point, but
Balthasar and Sequeri insist particularly on the shocking differentness of Christian revelation. It is never, they tell us, in easy continuity with our questions. It is interruption, rupture, excess. Its climax
in Cross and Resurrection takes us beyond all human logic. This is
a different realism, a disclosure that is never grasped by the merely

self-confident mind. What seems utterly impossible opens a door into risen life for us even here and now. But only a certain quality of desire and of receptive amazement makes this divine revolution possible.

For today's spiritual mood the Gospel can seem too good to be true. You know so much about the complexity of history that it seems naïve or impossible to say 'yes' to an old story of a preacher in Palestine. 'Can any good come out of Nazareth?' You can only find the answer by fidelity to other pillars of wisdom. For instance, if you approach this story with the quality of disposition seen in the fourth pillar, and if you live the active self-giving that will be the seventh pillar, you will be more ready for recognition of the figure of Jesus. There were moments in the Gospel when Jesus could not perform any miracles because familiarity bred closure and contempt. In her poem 'Praying', Mary Oliver invites us not to give priority to moments of intensity. Instead our best efforts bring us towards a possible recognition, to a doorway

> into thanks, and a silence in which
> another voice may speak.

Sixth pillar: Through a glass darkly

> I pray to God to rid me of 'God'.
> Meister Eckhart

This invites us to realise the sheer fragility of faith and of all our expressions of it. God is never obvious. Faith does not walk in steady and secure light. By all our usual standards of reality, God remains painfully unreal. The First Vatican Council evoked this darkness of faith, using some striking images: even after we recognise God's revelation, God remains 'shrouded in a veil' or 'enclosed in mist'.

This is the basis of what is called negative theology, reminding us that we need a certain humility in all our claims about God. It also reminds us that God remains painfully silent and strangely frustrating for our usual expectations. The young Joseph Ratzinger commented that Vatican II on atheism should have drawn more on this rich tradition, with its stress that God is always hidden, invisible, and transcendent. St Augustine had bluntly insisted, 'If you have understood, then it is not God ... If you think you have understood, your thought has deceived you'. St John of the Cross echoes this more positively: we encounter God better through 'not understanding than through understanding'. With typical lucidity, St Thomas Aquinas saw faith as an imperfect form of knowledge and therefore the believer's experience 'is akin to that of a doubter with suspicions'.

Your postmodern sensibility (as in Atwood's novel) can relish an ironic detachment from the Gospel. It rightly insists that God remains beyond all our ideas and images – ungrasped and ungraspable. But it is easy to confuse this wise reticence with agnosticism. The 'no' of an authentic negative theology comes after the 'yes' of faith. Being rooted in that 'yes' helps you to survive your struggles with the experience of 'no'. What are you to do with the heart of darkness (to echo a famous title of Conrad)? You run into shadows and emptiness. You may want to avoid them, but you know they are a crucial part of your human adventure.

In this light there can be a surprising convergence between agonised atheists and the dark journeys of the mystics. Both experience a strange 'unknowing'. Both of them diagnose a danger of creating God too cosily in our own image. The poet John Keats spoke of 'negative capability', a purified wisdom that you reach when you become 'capable of being in uncertainties, Mysteries, doubts, without any irritable reaching after fact and reason'.

Seventh pillar: Doing the Truth

> Any version of God out of tune
> with a movement of pure love is false.
> Simone Weil.

The Gospel of John says that whoever does the truth comes into the light (John 3:21). John's first letter points to a new epistemology: we know that we have passed from death into life when we love (1 John 3:14). Religious truth is not reached by roads of reflection alone but through how we live. Postmodern thinkers say that reality is 'performative' (a word also used by Pope Benedict concerning faith): we do not think ourselves into acting but act ourselves into different ways of understanding.

To quote again some insights from Wittgenstein: he once remarked to his Irish friend Maurice Drury that 'if you and I are to live religious lives, it mustn't be that we talk a lot about religion, but that our manner of life is different. It is my belief that only if you try to be helpful to other people will you in the end find your way to God'. He also wrote, 'Christianity is not a theory' but a way of life; 'practise gives the words their sense' and ultimately 'you have to change your life'.

We have heard this emphasis in several of our authors, certainly in Newman, Blondel, Soelle and O'Connor. 'We believe because we love', said Newman. Faith needs not just an inner disposition but an option for a different way of acting. It is only from within a lived commitment that it becomes alive. And since faith is more than an individual choice, this different life-style involves the community of believers. If the culture around is addicted to surfaces ('distracted from distraction by distraction', as T. S. Eliot put it), believers have to live from a different imagination, happily, visibly, and taking sides in the struggle for justice.

As a postmodern searcher for faith, have you ever encountered a living community of care? Such as those Christian groups who dedicate themselves to the marginalised or disabled, day in day out. More to the point, have you ever had real contact with the wounded of the world or tried to serve in this way? If not, your searching for spiritual meaning could lack an important note for its harmony. Think of that extraordinary moment in King Lear where a dictatorial old man reaches a language of humility. Reduced to 'houseless poverty' in the midst of a storm, he tells his two companions to go into the shelter ahead of him because he wants to 'pray'. In his meditation he realises that he had never really met suffering before, but now, in contact with the pain of others, he is free from unnecessary concerns and in fact closer to God.

> O, I have taken
> Too little care of this! Take physic, pomp;
> Expose thyself to feel what wretches feel,
> That thou mayst shake the superflux to them,
> And show the heavens more just.

Two key biblical statements have become incarnate here. Faith without works is dead. But a heart of stone can become a heart of flesh.

Towards 'more than we can imagine' (*St Paul*)

> All culminates at
> the threshold of Love,
> which only Love can cross.
> Jean-Luc Marion

'What is there more to say?' (Yeats). Much more remains, because *Deus semper maius*, God is always greater than our efforts to express or understand. As a well-known Zen saying puts it, the finger that points to the moon is not the moon itself. Faith finds its fullness not in what we say but in the reality of God. And where does that unreachable reality become real for us? As an encounter on the move. As a slow exodus from smallness, letting life be transformed by the Spirit.

A poem entitled 'Grace', by the Australian Judith Wright, begins:

> Living is dailiness, a simple bread
> That's worth the eating.

She goes on to evoke another presence, like a 'sudden laser' plunging into the ordinary. And she ends,

> Maybe there was once a word for it. Call it grace.
> I have seen it, once or twice, through a human face.

Our maps invite us beyond all our words into a Silence whose least unworthy name is Love: in fact Three Lovers loving us into loving – within our graced and wounded world of human faces.